THE WEALTH OF SALVATION
The PURPOSE, The PACKAGE, The PROMISE

CYNTHIA MCINNIS

Dedicated to new converts and backsliders who have found their way back home.

The memories of
Bishop Lawyer Carter and Deacon Daniel Carter
Prince of Peace Pentecostal Holiness Church

To Pastor Josephine Batts, Unity Prince of Peace Pentecostal Holiness Church, Brooklyn, NY and presently residing in Lawrenceville, VA

To Bishop and Elder Archie & Beverly McInnis, New Life Pentecostal Holiness Church

To Bishop Eric R. Figueroa, Sr.,
New Life Tabernacle, Brooklyn, NY

And to my Pastor, Bishop Archie L. McInnis, II
And my church, Full Effect Gospel Ministries

To my Mom, Mother Mary E. Johnson and my great family and to the memory of my brother, *Anthony Michael Johnson*

To the loving memory of my dad,
William Fenner,
"The Boy-scout",
who promised to meet me on the other side.

CHAPTER ONE: REDIRECTION
Big Fat "F" – Failure! Apology is Necessary

So, pick a state. Pick a community. Pick any daily news option or social media site and today you will find some reference to bold, outward racism, police brutality, murder, crime, politics and/or sexual perversion. It cannot be avoided. It's a cold world and very difficult to see that God is a real God.

Unfortunately, the subject or concept of God is not, at all, studied enough. If you ask any person walking down any street, what they know about God, very few, if any, will answer, "Nothing." You may hear that he is loving, real, kind, all-knowing, good, etc. You will most definitely get some very interesting dialogue about people's concept of God. In fact, the subject of God is the most known, but least studied concept amongst common people.

For the most part, people know what they have heard from others. This is fair enough, since we are talking about a God we cannot see; however, most of us have never seen George Washington either. The fact is, we know much of what we know about God and about others through books written about them. Even better, just as we can for George Washington and others, we can locate an autobiography and find out what God says about himself. Such a book, an autobiography of God, exists, but just like any other autobiography, we must believe that the author is indeed the author and that it is not the work of some creative writer with an equally creative agenda.

In order to study God we must believe that the Bible, the Koran or the Talmud is His autobiography. Since this book's primary focus is on the concept of Christ and Christianity, its references are to the Holy Bible as God's

1

autobiography. Please don't hang-up on me now! I have no desire to re-write the Bible or prove any points that faith alone cannot confirm, I am simply asking you, the reader, to look again.

According to the first verse of the Holy Bible, God made no attempt to prove his existence to us. He provided no lineage, no history of his past, no *begats*; he simply supplies, "In the beginning God"; proposing that in order to know him you must believe. Period. That's all you get. If you cannot accept Genesis 1:1 by faith, then reading the rest of the book is pointless.

My point here is that when there is reference material available, why rely heavily on the opinions of others? Read for yourself. Study for yourself. Find the most reputable source; one that has stood the test of time and from which countless other reference materials have evolved. For me, this is the Bible. My strongest ground here is my belief in, *2 Timothy 3:16, "All Scripture is given by inspiration of God, and is profitable for doctrine, for reproof, for correction, for instruction in righteousness:"* Of course, if you didn't believe Genesis 1:1, you would have never even found that one.

Having faith and believing in the Scripture seems to be the simplest way to knowing God right? But not! Something has gone terribly wrong. First of all, the Unbeliever would probably not know how to find, much less, believe 2 Timothy 3:16. How will they know God? OK! That's easy too right? The Believer can teach the Unbeliever – yes? Sadly, that is not always the case; as a matter of fact, when looking back in convoluted retrospect, from the beginning of the church to the church today, the Believer has done a poor job of teaching the Unbeliever who God is. We get a big fat "F"!

Please do not misunderstand me here. I am in no way saying that Satan is winning! I am also not saying that more souls have been won to Satan than to Christ. Really, how can anyone possibly know that? What I am emphatically saying is that for too many reasons and in too many ways, Believers have misrepresented Christ to the Unbeliever. I want to present some possible causes and then offer apologies on behalf of those Believers.

The main reason is that many of today's Christians do not really believe what we claim to represent. When the average American Christian of today is compared to the disciples and apostles of old, the concept of martyrdom, actually dying for what we believe, is a literal joke. For too many of us, we talk a good game but when it comes to real commitment to the faith we are the poster children for pitiful and the classic targets for world mockery.

Christianity, which was initially considered a respected lifestyle now appears to have become some watered-down religious concept and is the brunt of the world's jokes. It seems that whenever someone does not want to take responsibility for anything, or make a concrete stand for anything but wants to belong to something, they "join the Christian band."

"The ISIS regime has galvanized countless thousands in less than two years and the entire world takes them very seriously. Christians have been around for thousands of years yet the world does not take us seriously at all."
Michael Blue, CCFM Marion, South Carolina

As an ardent Apologist, defender of the faith, this is a very difficult stance for me to take, however, in order to begin to fix a problem, the true hard facts must be examined. While we must be constant at defending the faith, we can no longer afford to defend those who blatantly violate it.

It is, unfortunately, a thin line between "The Faith" and those who claim to represent it. There is an even thinner line between those who suffer failure and weakness but are doing their best to honor the Faith and those whose position is a blatant, "I don't care what people say about me. They have no heaven or hell to put me in."

For people like me, a book like this is truly risky business. Before I get to the next chapter, Luke 6:37 is already forming in the minds of some readers; *"Judge not, and ye shall not be judged: condemn not, and ye shall not be condemned: forgive and ye shall be forgiven:*

Knowing full well that my own intention is far from writing a book just to pass judgment on the people that belong to God, I must first agree with Luke 6:37 and then add John 7:24, *"Judge not according to appearance, but judge righteous judgment."* So then, to judge or not to judge is not the question, but to judge righteously (with a righteous intent) or with unrighteous intent is indeed our challenge.

Since this book is not about me, per se', I will not attempt to prove my intent. It will become evident as you continue to read. I only ask that you please continue to read.

I will, however, try to explain to you why I have stated that the church has failed to represent Christ properly over the years. I will share with you why I think the church of today gets a big fat "F" in Christ-like representation and then offer the necessary apologies on her behalf so that we may move forward toward repairing the breach and broadening the promised spread of salvation to those who are unsaved, angry, disappointed, frustrated, untrusting, even despising of what they think is the face of Christianity, the church or salvation today.

So, let's go ahead and get this out of the way shall we? Thanks!

MY APOLOGIES

If this applies to you, I apologize on behalf of every minister who has ever let you down. Whether he or she has been found in blatant acts of sin that directly violate the messages they have preached to others or lived a life before you that was an evident failure to mortify the deeds of the flesh.

I am almost certain that God covers those who are truly penitent and are suffocated by their own weaknesses and that the Holy Spirit guides, rebukes and admonishes until their faith is grown up enough to use the power freely granted to them. *Romans 8: 11 "But if the Spirit of him that raised up Jesus from the dead dwell in you, he that raised up Christ from the dead shall also quicken your mortal bodies by his Spirit that dwelleth in you. 12Therefore, brethren, we are debtors, not to the flesh, to live after the flesh. 13For if ye live after the flesh, ye shall die: but if ye through the Spirit do mortify the deeds of the body, ye shall live. 14For as many as are led by the Spirit of God, they are the sons of God."*

8: 26 "Likewise the Spirit also helpeth our infirmities: for we know not what we should pray for as we ought: but the Spirit itself maketh intercession for us with groanings which cannot be uttered."

Some, however, have clearly gone too far and stayed too long! Some have become so self-absorbed that they forgot you were watching; they didn't care that your faith was fragile and you needed an example in order to believe. I am sorry, please accept my apologies on their behalves and let's move forward, but this time, *"Looking unto Jesus the author and finisher of our faith; who for the joy that was set before him endured the cross, despising the shame, and is set down at the right hand of the throne of God." Hebrews 12:2*

Sexual immorality is at an all-time public high. Sex used to be private but has of late become the subject of very public controversy; sadly, this includes the "Christian" community. Of course, it also includes all faiths, creeds and communities, but again, this book is written on behalf of the Christian faith.

So let me continue my apologies on behalf of those Christians who suffer with the many facets of sexual immorality. The married leader who made several attempts to get you into his or her bed, the under-cover homosexual who lambasted you from the pulpit but met you privately behind closed doors, the so called Christian with the "door-knob" ministry, who just had to have everybody but told you that you were the only one, the creepy little pedophile who worked his or her way into your youth department and now you or your children are uncomfortable in their presence. While I cannot explain their actions and cannot accept weakness as a valid excuse, I apologize on their behalves.

I must reassure you that there is blood for sin and weakness, *1 John 1:9 "If we confess our sins, he is faithful and just to forgive us our sins, and to cleanse us from all unrighteousness."* Jeremiah 8:22, poses a question still asked today, *"Is there no balm in Gilead; is there no physician there? why then is not the health of the daughter of my people recovered?"* I reassure you that the answer is, "Yes!" There is a balm! There is help!

As real as your anger, pain, distrust or discomfort may be, and as real as your question may be, "Is there ever a leader that we can trust?" I assure you that there is someone in whom you can have total trust; His name is Jesus, our High Priest, *Hebrews 4:15 "For we have not an high priest which cannot be touched with the feeling of our infirmities; but was in all points tempted like as we are, yet without sin."*

Are you still with me? Good! By now you may have figured out that the beginning of enlightenment and understanding comes from prayer, healing, forgiveness and redirection! Pray and forgive everybody. *"And when ye stand praying, forgive, if ye have ought against any: that your Father also which is in heaven may forgive you your trespasses." Mark 11:25*

Accept my apologies on their behalves and redirect! We must redirect our focus away from finite man, who, although we have been given all things necessary for life and godliness, still manage to fail … *"According as his divine power hath given unto us all things that pertain unto life and godliness, through the knowledge of him that hath called us to glory and virtue:" 2 Peter 1:3* And direct our focus to our infinite Christ *"This then is the message which we have heard of him, and declare unto you, that God is light, and in him is no darkness at all. " 1 John 1:5*

Let us begin to consider the process of forgiveness and personal accountability so that we can move further in the book. Fair? Good, let's go further.

CHAPTER TWO: THE PURPOSE
"A ship is in a safe harbor, but that's not what ships are for" William Shedd

Understanding the purpose of a thing is quintessential to the proper use of a thing. I have heard it said, and agree, that if we misunderstand the purpose of a thing, we have a greater tendency to disregard or even abuse that thing. The example that was used for that concept was, understanding the purpose of wealth. When the purpose of wealth is misunderstood, money is often squandered, wasted and abused.

I will go further to say that while knowing *a* purpose for a thing is helpful, knowing God's purpose, or God's original intent for a thing is even better.

If a spouse does not understand God's purpose or original intent for marriage, the way it was originally designed, the same consequences are inevitable, disregard or abuse. But that, of course, is another book!

Before I make this attempt to share with you, the *wealth* of salvation, I think it is necessary to begin with its purpose, God's original intent; thus making you less susceptible to disregard or abuse it.

Because this writing is not an attempt at presenting a commentary on the subject but rather an approachable re-focus of it, I will not smother you with the many thousand Scripture verses on the topic but I must, for your sake, pull out a few and use others for your practical biblical reference.

9

One of those is, *Hebrews 2:3 "How shall we escape, if we neglect so great salvation; which at the first began to be spoken by the Lord, and was confirmed unto us by them that heard him;"*

I chose this one because it uses the word *escape*. The word *escape* implies urgency and desperation– after all, I have not heard of one prison escape where an escapee was found skipping or walking slowly away from the yard! Neither have I heard of one successful escape that was not well planned and taken very seriously.

I chose this verse because it feels like the writer and I share the same emotions about salvation. It must be considered seriously urgent and it must be well understood.

As you will read later, when we talk about *The Package,* I will discuss further flaws with the way we present salvation to unbelievers. I will stress, at this point, however that the subject of salvation is the main objective of the entire Bible and is so important that a man actually suffered a brutal, ignominious, horrible, bloody death to get it to us. Are we paying attention now?

Let us start at *our* beginning, (it is the safest starting point). In plain English, God created a world. There are countless theories as to His purpose for doing so. I will stick with the one I like most and that is, because he felt like it. Since I see God as the highest authority ever, I gladly accept that answer just as I did my parents' answer when I was bold enough to ask, "why?"; "Because I said so!" was their most often used response. Since God, In

Genesis 1:1, did not bother to give us a clear explanation for his purpose in creating the world, neither will I. Again, Genesis 1:1 says, *"In the beginning, God created the heavens and the earth"* it is not followed by the word, *because.*

Then God created people and placed them in a garden of the world he created; for this he gave very clear reasons and expressed his very clear intentions for them.

Genesis 2: 4.These are the generations of the heavens and of the earth when they were created, in the day that the LORD God made the earth and the heavens, 5And every plant of the field before it was in the earth, and every herb of the field before it grew: for the LORD God had not caused it to rain upon the earth, and there was not a man to till the ground. 6But there went up a mist from the earth, and watered the whole face of the ground. 7And the LORD God formed man of the dust of the ground, and breathed into his nostrils the breath of life; and man became a living soul."
Simply put, since there was no man to till the ground of the world he created, God made himself one.

Then he made a woman. *Genesis 2: 18And the LORD God said, It is not good that the man should be alone; I will make him an help meet for him. 19And out of the ground the LORD God formed every beast of the field, and every fowl of the air; and brought them unto Adam to see what he would call them: and whatsoever Adam called every living creature, that was the name thereof. 20And Adam gave names to all cattle, and to the fowl of the air, and to every beast of the field; but for Adam there was not found an help meet for him.*

In a very simple nutshell, the man had nothing suitable for himself and it was not good for him to be alone so God made a helper for him who was very much like himself and suitable for him. One of the major differences between the man and the helper was that the helper had a womb; there had to be a reason for that right? Of course there is!

God identifies the purpose or his original intent for putting the man and the woman together and making them *suitable* for each other, here in *Genesis 1:26, "And God said, Let us make man in our image, after our likeness: and let them have dominion over the fish of the sea, and over the fowl of the air, and over the cattle, and over all the earth, and over every creeping thing that creepeth upon the earth. 27So God created man in his own image, in the image of God created he him; male and female created he them. 28And God blessed them, and God said unto them, Be fruitful, and multiply, and replenish the earth, and subdue it: and have dominion over the fish of the sea, and over the fowl of the air, and over every living thing that moveth upon the earth. 29And God said, Behold, I have given you every herb bearing seed, which is upon the face of all the earth, and every tree, in the which is the fruit of a tree yielding seed; to you it shall be for meat. 30And to every beast of the earth, and to every fowl of the air, and to every thing that creepeth upon the earth, wherein there is life, I have given every green herb for meat: and it was so. 31And God saw every thing that he had made, and,*

*behold, it was very good. And the evening and the
morning were the sixth day.*

I want to pull out a few items from the above verses
and examine them a little further and make a point.
"Let them have dominion" – **"And God blessed
them, and God said unto them, Be fruitful, and
multiply, and replenish the earth, and subdue
it:"** **"*I have given* every green herb for meat."**

Now look at those verses and ask yourself, does it
look like there was any problem with anything that
was done? Did not God identify a potential problem
and solve it quickly by making a suitable helper for
the man? Did he supply every present and potential
need? Did he make his purpose – original intent for
mankind crystal clear? Was this not a perfect, fail-
proof plan?

God's original intent for man is to live without
need, in perfect harmony and communication with
him. Notice that I said God's intention *is,* not
God's intention *was*; this is because his intention
has not changed. If God's original intention has not
changed it is safe to assume that it would please him
to bring this to pass for us today.

Obviously, something *has* changed. We are not still
walking around happily butt naked in the Garden of
Eden, picking grapes and pomegranates. No sir, no
ma'am. Something has gone terribly wrong.

*(You may know this stuff already, but follow along
for the sake of those who may not. Indulge me.
Thanks!)*

13

With every purpose there must be a set of rules and/or guidelines to ensure its perfect, flawless continuance. For example, if you want more apples, you must continue to plant apple seeds, or if you want the land to continue to produce, you must continue to till the ground.

God's plan was perfect! Man had only to follow the guidelines to keep things going steadily. God knew this but God's enemy also knew this. If you go back to the paragraph that says, "let's start at *our* beginning", the word *our,* was not a typo. It is written that way on purpose; to let you know that there was a beginning before *our* beginning.

In a nutshell, before God began to begin our beginning, he had already begun a beginning somewhere else! Well, I'm cracking up about that but I'm so serious. There was always a heavenly existence. In the heavenly existence there were angels, one of which was a really special angel whose name was Lucifer. Apparently, this angelic superstar got *full of himself* in heaven and tried to exalt himself above God. It appears that God was, in no way, going to allow that! So, he kicked Lucifer out of heaven. *Isaiah 14:12,13 "How art thou fallen from heaven, O Lucifer, Son of the Morning! how art thou cut down to the ground, which didst weaken the nations! For thou hast said in thine heart, I will ascend into heaven, I will exalt my throne above the stars of God: I will sit also upon the mount of the congregation, in the sides of the north:"*

Again, I am not trying to write a commentary. I am trying to help you see the point. Period. Got it? Good! Now back to that garden.

What Satan, who was once called Lucifer, knew, was that God's plan for mankind is eternal and his word about it should be taken seriously. He also knew that God would never make anything or anyone that would be forced to serve him. It is always a matter of the will. God does not supersede will – not even an angel's, obviously! God wants to be loved. God wants to be chosen. He expects man to align his will with His word; after all, He knows what is best for us; He made us.

In order for all of the benefits he provided in the Garden to continue, man would have to "do" and "not do". Adam and Eve had the, *do,* part in-check but they had a problem with the, *not do,* part. *Genesis 2:15, "and the LORD God commanded the man, saying, Of every tree of the garden thou mayest freely eat: 17But of the tree of the knowledge of good and evil, thou shalt not eat of it: for in the day that thou eatest thereof thou shalt surely die."*

Unlike God in the beginning, He does not simply tell them not to eat of the specific tree but he also tells them why! He says to them, 'don't eat of this tree or else you will die.' Here is where things get twisted. It is not a part that can be ignored. It is vital to understand this, as it will lead us directly into the purpose of salvation. Are you still with me? Good!

Please know that although we understand death today as the separation from physical life, ashes to

15

ashes and dust to dust, etc. There was no such thing
in the Garden of Eden. Death, as we know it, was
never a part of God's original intention.

Satan was dead-set on continuing his plan to exalt
his kingdom above the kingdom of God. He wasted
no time. He used his cunning nature to work on one
of the very first of God's creations.

*Genesis 3: 1Now the serpent was more subtil than
any beast of the field which the LORD God had
made. And he said unto the woman, Yea, hath God
said, Ye shall not eat of every tree of the garden?
2And the woman said unto the serpent, We may eat
of the fruit of the trees of the garden: 3But of the
fruit of the tree which is in the midst of the garden,
God hath said, Ye shall not eat of it, neither shall ye
touch it, lest ye die. 4And the serpent said unto the
woman, Ye shall not surely die: 5For God doth
know that in the day ye eat thereof, then your eyes
shall be opened, and ye shall be as gods, knowing
good and evil. 6And when the woman saw that the
tree was good for food, and that it was pleasant to
the eyes, and a tree to be desired to make one wise,
she took of the fruit thereof, and did eat, and gave
also unto her husband with her; and he did eat.
7And the eyes of them both were opened, and they
knew that they were naked; and they sewed fig
leaves together, and made themselves aprons.*

Any good preacher could probably take this apart
and put it back together a thousand ways but I'm
not trying to preach to you, I'm trying to make sure
you understand exactly what is going on here. The
bottom line here is that Eve was deceived by a

trickery called *semantics: The study of meaning in language.*

He challenged God's meaning of the word *death* by saying, "you shall not *surely* die." Satan knew full well that Eve did not understand the term *die* to mean anything other than drop-dead or cease from living. What she understood was evidenced by what she added to God's words – "neither touch it." Touching and eating are both physical actions, which, to her knowledge, could only yield a physical result. While she understood the term *die,* she only understood it from a physical perspective. After all, she was bone of Adam's bone and flesh of Adam's flesh.

Satan, who was once a spirit, clearly knew what God meant and he was happy to share it knowing that she would be deceived by her own lust and that her lust would override her will. He knew that even truth is a challenge to lust!

He told her the absolute truth; God knew if they would eat from the forbidden tree, their eyes would be opened and they would know the difference between good and evil. I will add here that the greatest tactic in the game of deceit is the element of truth that is infused with it to make lies believable.

I will pause here to say that if you think I am deceived into believing that everyone who reads this book will be saved or will have a spiritual awakening and begin to live a life that is pleasing to God – just because they read this book, you are the one who is deceived! That doesn't even happen for everyone who reads the actual Bible. What I will tell you is this. Somebody will! That, my friend, is good enough for me.

And when the woman saw that the tree was good for food, and that it was pleasant to the eyes, and a tree to be desired to make one wise, she took of the fruit thereof, and did eat, and gave also unto her husband with her; and he did eat. 7And the eyes of them both were opened, and they knew that they were naked; and they sewed fig leaves together, and made themselves aprons.

We see here, the beginning of the fall of man and his introduction to the world, as we now know it. *"For all that is in the world, the lust of the flesh, and the lust of the eyes, and the pride of life, is not of the Father, but is of the world." 1 John 2:16*

Lust: to be eager for something; desire. You see all three of these in Eve's responses to Satan's influence. While she knew the truth, she failed in her battle against, *"all that is in the world"*. She saw that it was good for food (The lust of the flesh). She noticed that it was pleasant the eyes (The lust of the eyes). And finally, she recognized that it was a tree to be desired to make one wise (The pride of life). Hook, line and sinker! Just like that, a perfect plan appeared to be destroyed forever. Satan really did some damage that day.

Gee whiz! All this drama for a little bite of a piece of fruit? Really? This all seems so extreme right? Let me share with you why their actions proved to be so devastating. You see, death was not the only thing that was not in God's original plan for

mankind, neither was sin. Their disobedience to
God was a sin against God, not to mention, an
insult; Eve's choice to obey Satan rather than the
words of God and Adam's choice to obey his wife
(whom God provided for him) rather than the voice
of God is a clear sign that they had been deceived!

Sin altered the state of mankind forever. Big
mistake! So, God levied out punishments, like any
good father would but he did not leave them
standing there naked. He covered them. It's what
God does. He makes provision for our inadequacies.
Although he was displeased with their decisions, he
loved them just the same. He remained God, their
father.

*Genesis 3:22, 'And the LORD God said, Behold, the
man is become as one of us, to know good and evil:
and now, **lest he put forth his hand, and take also
of the tree of life, and eat, and live for ever:"***

The section highlighted is, indeed, the purpose for
salvation. Since the man disobeyed God's command
and sin had altered his state, Satan's next attempt
would be to get him to eat from the Tree of Life.
Doing so would cause him to live forever in the
sinful state in which he had now occupied. There
would be no hope for man ever regaining an
acceptable relationship with his God. God would
always love him but the man would not be able to
love Him back! Sin would forever drive a wedge
between mankind and God. *"Behold, the LORD'S
hand is not shortened, that it cannot save; neither
his ear heavy, that it cannot hear:*

19

2 But your iniquities have separated between you and your God, and your sins have hid his face from you, that he will not hear." Isaiah 59:1,2

But our loving God had a plan! He would not let this happen. *Genesis 3:"23 Therefore the LORD God sent him forth from the garden of Eden, to till the ground from whence he was taken. 24 So he drove out the man; and he placed at the east of the garden of Eden Cherubims, and a flaming sword which turned every way, to keep the way of the tree of life."* God put them out of paradise for their own good.

Notice that God placed an angel and a flaming sword to keep the way of the tree of life. It shows how much he loved mankind. God always makes provision for protection from the forbidden. To the Unbeliever, he uses the Believer who is filled with the fire of the Holy Ghost, strapped and available for His use.

As, I mentioned. Much punishment was doled out to the man for his disobedience to God. As it was then, so it is now. But I sure don't want you to think that Satan/the serpent got away from God's punishment. No sir! No ma'am!

Genesis 3:15, Gives some very interesting insight as to the plan of salvation. *"14 And the LORD God said unto the serpent, Because thou hast done this, thou art cursed above all cattle, and above every beast of the field; upon thy belly shalt thou go, and dust shalt thou eat all the days of thy life:"*

Now the serpent could no longer stand up but had to slither on his belly and shut his mouth. God spared the serpent because Satan was merely using it. It was not in the nature of the serpent to deceive man. God created him with all the other creeping things.

But things do not go so well for Satan here.

3:15 And I will put enmity between thee and the woman, and between thy seed and her seed; it shall bruise thy head, and thou shalt bruise his heel.

From the surface, it appears that God is merely referring to Eve when he mentions the woman but then God mentions, *seed*. What seed? What head? What heel?

When God says, "I will put enmity…" he means that there will be eternal hostility between Satan and Jesus Christ. Satan will never be saved. He is incapable of ever receiving Jesus Christ as Savior. Christ and Satan will remain eternally exclusive. This does not only refer to Satan but also to all who are begotten of him. His seed. His cohorts, his spawn, and his demons will remain in eternal hostility with Christ.

The seed of the woman is Jesus Christ. The seed of the woman is followed closely throughout the entire Bible so that the lineage of Christ can be traced directly back to Eve. Scholars and theologians have carefully followed the seed of the woman to show how God's divine providence would protect this seed from all of the attacks of the enemy.

By saying, *"it shall bruise thy head, and thou shalt bruise his heel.* God is predicting the defeat of Satan by the coming of Christ, the Messiah.

"He shall bruise your head" is a mortal wound. The cross of Christ eternally crushes the power of Satan! Before we ever knew anything about a cross, God shows us here that he already had a plan for salvation. God promises a solution to their sin. At the fall Satan bruised the heel of Jesus. Sin was the cause of Christ going to the cross. At the cross Christ will crush Satan's head. One is a non-lethal and the other a lethal act. At the cross Jesus dealt Satan a fatal blow. There he paid for the penalty of sin fully.

Christ not only paid for the sins of the world on the cross but he defeated Satan there. *Colossians 2: 14, "Blotting out the handwriting of ordinances that was against us, which was contrary to us, and took it out of the way, nailing it to his cross; 15And having spoiled principalities and powers, he made a shew of them openly, triumphing over them in it."* Satan was executed at the cross.

"And you shall bruise His heel" refers to the death of Christ. Whether this refers literally to the heels of Jesus pressed against the cross, is not important. Jesus was bruised at the cross, *Isaiah 53:10, "Yet it pleased the Lord to bruise him; he hath put him to grief: when thou shalt make his soul an offering for sin, he shall see his seed, he shall prolong his days, and the pleasure of the Lord shall prosper in his hand."*

The theme of Genesis 3:15 is reiterated throughout the entire Bible. Through much hard work and countless years of Biblical study, the entire plan of salvation can be clearly seen throughout the chapters of the Bible.

I want you to remember and consider often the suffering of our savior, Jesus Christ.

"Wherefore seeing we also are compassed about with so great a cloud of witnesses, let us lay aside every weight, and the sin which doth so easily beset us, and let us run with patience the race that is set before us, 2Looking unto Jesus the author and finisher of our faith; who for the joy that was set before him endured the cross, despising the shame, and is set down at the right hand of the throne of God. 3For consider him that endured such contradiction of sinners against himself, lest ye be wearied and faint in your minds." Hebrews 12:2,3

Jesus' eventual death would be bloody, painful, excruciating and humiliating. He would suffer, bleed and die all to assure that mankind is forever freed from the penalty of sin. Man needs only to believe in his heart and confess what he believes and his present state of sin, *Romans 5:12, "Wherefore, as by one man sin entered into the world, and death by sin; and so death passed upon all men, for that all have sinned"* is supernaturally transferred back to God's original intent; he shall be saved!

Romans 9: "That if thou shalt confess with thy mouth the Lord Jesus, and shalt believe in thine heart that God hath raised him from the dead, thou

23

shalt be saved. 10For with the heart man believeth unto righteousness; and with the mouth confession is made unto salvation. 11For the scripture saith, Whosoever believeth on him shall not be ashamed. 12For there is no difference between the Jew and the Greek: for the same Lord over all is rich unto all that call upon him. 13For whosoever shall call upon the name of the Lord shall be saved."

If you are reading this chapter and you are not saved, please allow me to take this time to offer you the greatest gift ever to have been given unto men! Salvation.

CHAPTER THREE – THE PACKAGE
A person wrapped up in himself makes a small package.- Harry Emerson Fosdick

I have heard it said that the greatest trick the devil has ever played on mankind was to make them believe he does not exist. While I believe that entirely, I believe that he has played and even bigger trick on the world.

Satan has created a masterminded plan to alter the packaging of sin in such a way that its harmful spiritual effects were made mundane and its pleasurable, social benefits were ideal. He has, in fact, turned a mountain into a molehill. Let me show you what I mean.

Consider the big-business tobacco companies that sell cigarettes. From the on-set, everyone involved knew that cigarette smoking was detrimental to your health. There was no question about that. They knew that the ingredients used to create cigarettes were poisonous and would, without doubt, cause cancer. Yet, they have been able to sell the world on it!

It was the packaging. No halfway intelligent business mind would ever try to sell a product by exacerbating its devastating effects, so, like the serpent in the garden, some aspect of truth must be used to draw the suckers in.

Cigarette smoking was *packaged* as a social must-have. Every one who was someone, was smoking. Television stars from leading ladies to debonair sex symbols to hard-core gangsters like, Humphrey

Bogart, Bette Davis and James Cagney characters were all constant smokers. Daily commercials showing moms pushing baby carriages, stopping to chat in the playground were smoking. Athletes and Catholic priests, all smokers.

Cigarette smoking was packaged in such a way that there could not possibly have been anything wrong with them. By the time, people would notice or pay any attention to the required notification, "Warning: The Surgeon General has determined that cigarette smoking is harmful to your health"; stamped in the smallest font and placed in the most obscure place on the package, the damaging affects had already begun. Tobacco is extremely addictive. So the people were hooked!

Without a doubt, Satan has repackaged sin to make the warning as small, insignificant and obscure as possible; "The wages of sin is death ...BUT THE GIFT OF GOD IS ETERNAL LIFE". He has glamorized sin and made it pleasurable. As the years have gone by, sin is becoming more and more welcoming than ever. Let's take a look back over just a few years ago.

Do you remember, "I Love Lucy"? Or, "The Honey-Mooners?" Both television shows were based around two married couples that were close friends. They were married but have you ever seen them sleep together and if so, in the same bed? When they referred to pregnancy the term was, "having a baby." – Let's go further, did you ever see an episode where either of them ever committed adultery? Have you ever seen Fred push-up on Lucy on the low? What about Ralphy-boy? Have you ever seen him stare at Ed Norton inappropriately? Did Little Ricky have fantasies about his friend Davy? By now I think you have gotten my point. If you're under fifty and have not seen these shows, watch Nick at Night or take my word for it – the answer to every question is a blaring, "NOPE!"

As time has gone by, Satan has amped up his packaging of sin to be more glamorous than ever. He is drawing in one new sucker at a time. He has made his way into the media, the music industry and the all-mighty Internet. Saying, Martin and Gina are not married but they have sex all day, every day. The rappers only make money if they glamorize murder and illicit sex, female artists who bare all, purchase bigger breasts and backsides have a better shot than any other.

Rebellion is major in this day – even though the Bible describes it as – witchcraft. Satan has sold himself as being mightier than God and he was such a good salesman that men and women are selling their souls to him more than the average person will ever know. He packaged himself as money; Lots and lots of money. He packaged himself as fame; world recognition, lofty positions. In essence, he has packaged his major product as one that would take you to the top of the world.

He has gone much further than the cigarette industry. He has added designer drugs, alcohol, prescription drugs and even household cleaning products.

Oh, these, by far are the least of His tactics. Because he is a spirit, he is able to infiltrate the

27

minds and manipulate the emotions causing mental addictions, like pornography and sexting; Sex-calls and wet dreams. He has gone as far as mentally convincing men and women to feel like another gender is trapped inside of them. It is emotional manipulation to its greatest extent. It is a psychological addiction so strong that it actually has people surgically removing their body parts, altering their clothing and body movements. It is a manipulation easily recognizable through the eyes and body language so that it appears to be an orientation and not a choice. It is not an orientation and neither is it a choice it is a carefully planned satanic manipulation of the mind and emotions. The entire LGBT community is absolutely right when they say they have not chosen to be as they are; they have all been mentally and emotionally manipulated and raped by Satan.

He has a bigger plan than most of us can see. If Satan has chosen a vice to usher in the physical Antichrist, this one is it! Have you noticed that the world is silent on most issues except the LGBT agenda? If you don't believe me, try to offend them in the least possible way and the whole world goes crazy. If Satan needs a group to mobilize to push any of his agendas, he has one!

If you want to win a political race, play to the LGBT agenda. If you want to get attention, make a public statement for or against LGBT. I submit to you that while Satan has no power to kill, he has the power of suggestion that will cause you to kill yourself before you ever get to read the warning labels.

The Bible has been around as long, in fact, longer than any of Satan's devices. It contains the warning labels and the cure for addictions, yet people still gravitate to sin. Just like they got hooked on cigarettes, the world has become hooked on sin.

Sadly, Satan has yet another trick up his sleeve! He would manipulate the minds of Christian Believers and lull them to sleep on the warning labels and cause them to only see the social, glamorous, happy side of Christianity. Like the cigarette companies he magnifies the church as a place for marriages and christenings, picnics and food programs and put the sin labels somewhere on the very bottom, written in small print. He has done this by silencing the church about sin.

Finally, after far too many years, and countless millions of cigarette addictions, someone has decided not to keep silent any more. Someone who had a passion for those who were dying miserable, horrible slow deaths at the hands of cigarette smoking has decided to mobilize a group to fight against it.

Now we see that public advertisement of cigarettes and cigarette smoking has decreased and sickening commercials showing the effects of this deadly product are on the rise. They have finally re-packaged cigarette smoking but sadly it is too little, too late.

"For the wages of sin is death..." Romans 6:23 Why would people continue in the behaviors that only produce death? Why would people choose one who comes to steal, kill and destroy? *"The thief*

cometh not, but for to steal, and to kill, and to destroy:" John 10:10 We have been warned! *"Be sober, be vigilant; because your adversary the devil, as a roaring lion, walketh about, seeking whom he may devour:" 1 Timothy 5:8* – yet people are drawn to him by the billions!

We must mobilize our forces to re-package sin and then, unfortunately, we must also re-package salvation. Yes! We have much work to do and the time is always right now.

The church you see today is unfortunately very close to or in fact in a sad state of Apostasy. Too many of us have been hushed by the will of the world. We have been purchased with the same currency as the world. For too many preachers, super-star status exceeds the desire for truth and soul-to-soul ministry. The desire for mega-churches has clouded our desire for mega soul winning so we have made church-going a popularity choice and not the planting of the Lord.

Before you start, sadly there is a need for this disclaimer. I am not mega-church opposed. Who does not want a big church, filled with people and full parking lots? I celebrate the ministries that are financially able to do the great commission and the Lord's work because of the member-based contributions. The truth is, *Luke 14:23 says, "And the lord said unto the servant, Go out into the highways and hedges, and* **compel** *them to come in, that my house may be filled."* So, I am not against a full house.

It is what is being taught or not being taught inside of that house that attributes to the state of the church today. If we do not make public declarations against sin and worldliness and all that is in the world, how will they know what to be wary of? How will sin ever be repackaged? How will people be able to make God-conscious decisions?

I cannot talk about repackaging sin without considering that we repackage salvation. Unfortunately, there is almost as much sin in our pulpits as is in the world. Something has gone wrong. In earlier chapters I offered apologies on the behalf of those who have let us down because of sin, now I want to make an attempt to change the packaging of salvation back to what it was originally.

Salvation, Christianity and the church have all been repackaged to be synonymous terms. People can either say, I am saved, a born-again Christian or a church-goer and it almost sounds like the exact same thing. Well, I take issue with that because of the present state of the church.

Major weight has been taken away from what is the central theme of the entire Bible. Jesus Christ died the excruciating, humiliating; debilitating death by crucifixion to get salvation to us! Its wealth cannot be diluted by semantics!

To turn the hearts of men back to God we must both repackage sin and salvation. We must first show God, the Father in creation, who devised a plan of salvation in the beginning of time and watched over his word to perform it in the fullness of time. A God

31

who loved mankind so much that he would not allow us to die in sin without a remedy. We must not leave out that this loving God, creator of mankind absolutely hates sin because he knows, full well, the devastating affects it has on the lives of His people. He knows that sin is the major playing tool of his enemy, the devil; it is his best card drawn to play, manipulate and bamboozle mankind out of his Godly inheritance, salvation! God hates sin.

We must first show Christ as the savior of the world who loved us so much that he took the pain and bore our sin. He was born and walked among mankind. He experienced hurt and pain; suffering and temptation; betrayal and denial just to cleanse us from all unrighteousness.

We must not be so quick to drop Christ on someone and send him on his way. Jesus wants to be chosen. He wants to be loved. This takes time. He said, *"Take my yoke upon you, and learn of me; For I am meek and lowly in heart and you shall find rest unto your souls" Matthew 11:29*

Does that sound like someone who wants a one-night-stand? He wants a life-long relationship with us. He wants us to get to know him for real. He does not want us to ignore what he hates! What kind of relationship are you in if you don't know what the person you're with hates? You cannot just know what he loves, you must also know what he hates. Jesus hates sin.

Let's look at relationship like this; Say you're in a relationship with one person but decide to have a fling with another. Now say you and this other decide to go to a hotel to *do the wild thing* –but you found out when you got there that the one you're in a relationship with is already in the hotel room when you got there. Would you proceed to that wild thing? Of course not! You are not trying to hurt the person you're in relationship with- you were just "doing you"- or at least about to do you.

Can you imagine how that person would feel to know that he or she has given all he could to the relationship, yet you want someone else? He would hate that. Well, in salvation, Jesus Christ has come into your heart so it's not like you can do anything behind his back. Anything you do is right in his face. Would you participate in what he hates, right in his face? That, my friend, is real relationship. Not a watered down version of semantics.

Salvation must be packaged as the most valuable asset you can ever attain. You want nothing to compromise it. So that you do not live the way you live as if you're a prisoner bound by bands that restrict your free movement but you live as a person who is loyal to one who has been loyal; as a person who makes sacrifices on behalf of one who has made even greater sacrifices for you; as one who loves even as one who has been loved first.

There is no set of rules for that. Jesus says, *"He that hath my commandments, and keepeth them, he it is that loveth me: and he that loveth me shall be loved of my Father, and I will love him, and will manifest myself to him." John 14:21*

The prerequisites for falling in love with Jesus are right here in Verse 21. *"He that hath my commandments...*" To begin with, you must have his word. You must know it. What is the big rush? Take your time and *learn of him.* No one gets into a relationship on Monday and falls in love on Tuesday. Infatuation maybe, but love takes time. Jesus wants to be loved so he opens himself up to us first. This is me! You can find out everything you need to know about me in this book – the whole book is about me.

Don't be sidetracked or distracted by the people who represent or misrepresent him.

Get to know him for yourself. To know him is to love him! Satan will have you distracted by this life's worries. Money to pay bills, person-to-person relationships, personal social status and whatever but Matthew 6:33 will help you understand the wealth of salvation; it says, *"But seek ye first the Kingdom of God, and His righteousness and all thee things shall be added unto you".*

You must see salvation as a Kingdom idea! Kingdoms have riches and treasures. Your enemy wants you to be so busy fighting denominations, doctrines, issues and each other that, like the Pharisees, you don't see the loving Savior standing right in front of you. He wants you to be so distracted by the "people of God" that you ignore the Savior's invitation that says, *"Come unto me ..."* He never said come unto *my people* or even come unto *my church.*

The second prerequisite is to keep the commandments. *"He that hath **my commandments**, and **keep**eth them, he it is that loveth me ..."* - this

34

is what people do that love him. Love is shown by living a life that pleases the one you love.

So many people in the two other categories; Church-goers and Born-again Christians, use these titles but fail to live lives that please Christ. Our lives must be in alignment with God's word in order to please him. Pleasing God requires a complete *will alignment.*

While I live in a no-judgment zone for the most part, I cannot help but believe that Satan has repackaged salvation to look like lifestyle does not matter; but it is lifestyle that people see. They cannot see our hearts. The love for God in our hearts should be reflected in our lifestyles so that others will desire him.

Falling in love with Jesus is the best thing any of us can ever do. Do you remember really being in love? You forsook all others for the one you loved. You made time to be with the one you loved. You adjusted your lifestyle for the one you loved. You did things you would not ordinarily do for the sake of the one you loved. Love does that to you.

These days when we hear about the love of God it is so one-sided. God loves all people; God looks beyond our faults; God blesses all people. We hear what God does because he loves us but when are we going to hear what we do because we love him? The world cannot see what God does for us but they can see what we do for God. They can see when the things we used to do, we don't do any more and the places we used to go, we don't go any more – Why? Because we love Jesus! They can see us adjust our lifestyles from retaliating to forgiving and forgetting. They can see us handle our struggles and proclivities through prayer, fasting and self-denial. They can see us *change.*

This is how Jesus must be packaged! He must be packaged as someone to love not just someone to serve. To know him is to love him *and* to love him is to serve him. True servant-hood is birthed out of love. When a person serves because he loves, his service is warm, welcoming and received.

There are too many people serving in the churches that do not love Jesus. Oh, they say they love him, but their lifestyles displease him. What kind of love is that? They might like him but they have not spent enough time with him to fall in love.

They walked into the church and started working in the church. They think they're serving the Lord, when, in fact, they are merely serving the church. They do not attend Sunday-School classes or Bible Study and are often so busy *serving* that they do not listen to the preacher. This is sure-fire way to clearly misrepresent our loving Savior. They cannot get to know him that way!

I want to repackage salvation to be something that all men desire. Not as a life sentence for those who are guilty and have no other choices. Not as a part of our life that we are too ashamed to admit to. Not as the hidden factor that only comes out when questioned.

There is a wealth *inside* of salvation that must be known. Every answer to every one of life's questions is *in* salvation. Once a person is saved for real, the wealth of salvation is revealed. Salvation must be packaged as a life-long journey, not a one-shot–deal. It is not a hit-it-and-quit-it decision like what is done at the rehearsed altar calls that require a person to repeat a few sentences, shake a few hands and walk away, never to be seen again.

We must begin the process of packaging and re-packaging salvation because it should not be difficult to give away the best thing in life, for free.

CHAPTER FOUR
THE PROMISE

"Keep every promise you make
and only make promises you can keep" Anthony Hitt

When considering promises, the most important factor is not merely what is being promised but *who* is making the promise. A promise most intriguing is nothing more than wishful thinking when made by an unreliable source.

Jesus makes this very interesting promise in Matthew 11:28-30, "Come unto me, all ye that labour and are heavy laden, and I will give you rest. Take my yoke upon you, and learn of me; for I am meek and lowly in heart: and ye shall find rest unto your souls. For my yoke is easy, and my burden is light."

One thing is immediately evident; if you want to benefit from the promise he has made, you must first come and get it! The promise begins with, "come unto me." You must leave one place and arrive at another place. In order to do that, you must trust the promise maker enough to bust a move!

The wisest thing for an enemy to do, if he does not want you to receive that which is promised, is to keep you from getting to the promise maker. An enemy that knows the promise maker well enough to know that if you do as he has asked, you will definitely receive what he has promised, will do whatever he can do to keep you from him.

The promise is, "I will give you rest". Jesus makes it clear that what he has promised is a gift. It is not something that can be merited. Why wouldn't Satan want you to have *rest?*

Amazingly, the Holy Spirit had me to stop at the question above. I just stopped typing. I did not know why. Our God is amazing! Most anointed writers know that when the pen flow stops – you stop. You do not always know why. In this case I had to wait for inspiration, particularly a prophetic impartation.

It occurred that recently we had an unscheduled service. Bishop George Bloomer called my husband to say that he was led of the Lord to come to our church; he had a prophetic impartation for our ministry, particularly, the Allentown, PA location where I am privileged to be the resident Associate Pastor.

His message was about giving God his Sabbath with Sabbath meaning rest. He shared that the Sabbath, or *rest* in this sense of the word rest means to cease from labor used to earn income, not necessarily resting from anything that makes you tired. His example was that if you are vacationing and enjoying yourself, you often come home so tired that you need another vacation.

Giving God his Sabbath means that you rest from the labor used to earn money to live and to give God his time in worship, prayer and devotion.

It gets better, Bishop Bloomer shared the Scripture verse, 2 Chronicles 36:21 *"To fulfill the word of the Lord by the mouth of Jeremiah, until the land had enjoyed her Sabbaths; for as long as she lay desolate she kept Sabbath, to fulfill threescore and ten years."* His explanation of this verse astonished me to the point that I am led of the Lord to share it with you.

Bishop Bloomer says that this verse implies that as long as the land lay desolate – as long as there was no production, no growth, no harvest, the land was able to *give God his Sabbath* or she kept Sabbath. He went further to explain that God will get his Sabbath from us whether we want to give it to him or not. Even if he has to force it on us, he will then bless us for it!

So that, there will be no productivity, no increase and no harvest to the land or the person who holds back God's Sabbath! God wants his time. He says, the land is not cursed, although it appears desolate, although it appears to be in a famine, it rests awaiting the *right person* to till it and wake it from its rest.

It will take a person, a group of persons who are *up-to-date* on God's Sabbaths to wake up a seemingly barren land! The same concept applies to tithers but that is another story.

So, back to the question, why would Satan try to keep you from the promise, "and I will give you rest"? If Satan can keep you so financially oppressed, laboring and heavy laden that you do not have time or are just too worn out to give God His Sabbath, he knows that you will be going around in circles expecting a land to produce that will not produce for you.

Once Satan gets you oppressed with the cares of this life he knows your relationship with God will suffer! He knows that you will not take the time to seek God and build a real relationship with him. He will encourage you to find churches with shorter worship times, no pressure about lifestyle and watered down Bible Study. He will re-direct your thinking from giving God quality worship to finding out how much money is in God's prosperity plan for you.

Why? Because you are oppressed, stressed out and barely making it financially.

Satan will never tell you that your ground is not producing because you are too over-extended to give God his tenth or because you are too busy hustling to give God the time he requires. Why would he do that? If he does you will get the promise, *"and I will give you rest!"*

He needs you oppressed with stress and lack so that he can force you into depression. Surely, if you stay oppressed long enough, depression will follow. It is in the depression stage that most alcoholics, drug addicts, pornographers, adulterers and fornicators are made. Oppression leads to depression. There is no rest for your soul when you are oppressed and there is little concern for your soul when you are depressed. You begin to feel that God does not exist and if he does exist he certainly does not care about what you are facing. It's a trick of the enemy! It's another one of Satan's strategies to trick you out of your promise. Just like Jacob offered Esau food when he was famished, the devil will offer you alternatives when you are oppressed but don't you dare go for it!

If you are reading this book, saved or unsaved, Believer or Unbeliever and you are experiencing burn-out, stress, oppression or depression you should stop and give your God a praise because he strategically got this book into your hands and stopped the devil from distracting you from reading this chapter! Oh yeah! He's good like that!

He promised you rest for your souls! He promised to remove the yoke of bondage from your neck and replace it with his yoke – the yoke (the commitment to him) that is easy. He promised to remove your heavy burden of

41

oppression and replace it with his burden (the call to service for him) that is light.

Satan knows full well that this will NEVER happen if you do not first, *"Come to Him"*. To come to Christ is a conscious and deliberate walking away from Satan, his influence, his suggestions and his thoughts and to come to Christ's consciousness by the renewing of your mind. "Let this mind, be in you, that was also in Christ Jesus." Philippians 2:5

Once you accept Jesus Christ as your savior you receive his spirit inside of you. Satan knows this better than you do. He will do whatever he can to prevent this because once the spirit of Christ is in you it is impossible for him to use his final weapon against you; after oppression is left unchecked, Satan influences depression; after depression is left unchecked, he influences his final weapon and that is possession!

Remember, Satan is a spirit, so, although the television shows people throwing up green stuff and spooky images going into and out of bodies, remember that is movie drama! The real deal is that after Satan has been able to manipulate your mind through oppression and depression, he needs only to take is a step further for possession as long as the spirit of Christ does not dwell in you.

I have seen Satan spiritually manipulate the mind to the point where he makes them believe that he is inside of them throwing them around, slamming them to the floor, lifting them up from the ground, slithering like a snake, speaking though their mouths in different voice tones, scratching and cutting themselves. That is when he is showing off and trying to scare others into believing what they are seeing.

The truth is, Jesus says, *"Behold, I give you power to tread upon serpents and upon scorpions and OVER ALL THE POWER OF THE ENEMY, and nothing shall by any means hurt you." Luke 10:19*

Satan is a bully to the weak and the biblically illiterate. He will use tactics of persuasion to manipulate the word of God when he has the mind of a Believer, just as he did Eve in the Garden. He is smooth enough to get you to say what he is saying and not what you know is right.

In his conversation with Eve, he refers to God in the masculine, noble term, Elohim. By this time, Eve and Adam had been in an intimate and close personal relationship with God and referred to Him as "YhWh" (Lord God, intimating personal and intimate relationship) but by the conversation's end, Eve was referring to God as "Elohim" – just like the serpent. While we cannot readily see that in the English version of the Bible, each time it says GOD; but with a little advanced study you will see that words that sound the same do not always mean the same things in Scripture.

You are reading this book and, trust me, Satan is horrified and ticked-off right now because his tactics and manipulative devices are challenged and uncovered. You are becoming more empowered and less likely to be bullied by a defeated devil!

Jesus says, "Behold!" – recognize and believe, I promise you that when you come to me I will give you power over the devil and rest for your soul.

It is only when your soul is at rest that you build confidence in God's promises and his ability. I often refer to the swimmer's contrast with floating when I say as long as you are swimming you are using your arms, your legs and your breathing mechanisms to stay afloat. You are not at rest. You are working. You will soon develop the self-confidence required to become a better and better swimmer. You are relying on your own efforts and your own abilities to swim. Floating is a different concept altogether. Floating is not swimming. Floating is resting in the confidence that the water can hold you! God wants us to swim to develop self-confidence but he wants us to float to develop God-confidence.

Your soul is at rest when you are confident in God's promises and his ability, even if you do not know his plan, you know his promise and that He is fully able to keep every promise he has made to you.

Admittedly, of all the promises Jesus has made to us concerning Salvation, I had no idea why God gave me this one to elaborate on, but I know now! Eternal life is the ultimate promise of salvation but we cannot focus on the eternal when we live in the now. Satan has no power in the eternal; he can only work now!

I am so tired of seeing God's people face defeat after defeat because they do not know the tactics of Satan or are so weak that he can manipulate their minds and play them like a clarinet. If we can ever take the time to step out of his maze and look around, we will see that he uses the same methods and tactics over and over, since the beginning of time.

His main motive is to get you to focus on anything other than the promises of God for your life; those promises are found in God's word.

Come to Jesus! Come to Him for real. Walk away from the world. This is true salvation. Empty yourself of any characteristic of Satan through sanctification and trust God for His promise, "And I will pray the Father, and he shall give you another Comforter, that he may abide with you forever; even the Spirit of truth; whom the world cannot receive, because it seeth him not, neither knoweth him: but ye know him; for he dwelleth with you, and shall be in you." John 14:16-17 – Receive His promise and be filled with the Holy Ghost.

CONCLUSION
The Wealth of Salvation

"How shall we escape, if we neglect so great salvation;
which at first began to be spoken by the Lord, and was
confirmed unto us by them that heard him;" Hebrews 2:3

The term "wealth" as defined, makes every reference to the
abundance of valuable possessions or money. It is also
defined as the state of being rich; material prosperity,
plentiful supplies of a particular resource or a plentiful
supply of a particular desirable thing.

Many of you may have been disappointed that you have
reached the conclusion of this book but have not read how
to find the money! The following passages may help with
that!

The Old Testament. All wealth originally formed part of
God's good creation, over which humans were given
dominion (Gen 1:26). This responsibility remained
after the fall (9:1-3), but sin corrupted the process. God
promised to make a great nation of Abraham's
offspring, centered around prosperity in the promised
land (12:7 ; 15:18 ; 17:8 ; 22:17). The patriarchs
themselves were wealthy, as a first token of this
blessing from God (24:35 ; 26:13 ; 30:43). So too God
materially blessed the Israelites in Goshen as a
testimony to the Egyptians (47:27). En route to
Canaan, however, God very clearly places stipulations
on the accumulation of wealth; manna and quail were to
be collected so that no one had too little or too much.
Exod 16:16-18 ; quoted in 2 Cor 8:15).
http://www.biblestudytools.com/dictionary/wealth/

I would like to focus primarily on the term, "valuable possession." While religion, church-going and spirituality are terms that refer to parts of our lives, I want to stress that salvation is the most valuable possession of our lives.

The beginning of the book clearly contrasts the differences between salvation and religious affiliation, church attendance and spirituality and show that while those references really enhance our present lives, salvation creates a brand new life and renders us citizens of an entirely different Kingdom! We are in this world but not *of* this world. John 15:19

In order to see the great wealth that is salvation, we must not view it as an added part of our lives but the ultimate "fix" for a broken mess that we did not cause; a mess so, intertwined and complicated that it took 66 books to explain it, a bloody death to correct it and countless preacher's to unravel it!

Salvation comes at the great price of shed blood, from the cross to the last martyr in 2016! It continues to cost the lives of those who understand its value to the point that they refuse to compromise it even if the face of imminent death. Why? Why would they die for it? Clearly they understand the value of it! It means more than life to them. If this is not your testimony; and I do not mean what you say, but truly who you are, then this book was for you.

It is my desire that whoever reads this uncovers the hidden wealth that is salvation and embraces it as fully as the treasure that it is. "But we have this treasure in earthen vessels, that the excellency of the power may be of God, not of us." 2 Corinthians 4:7

Do not contaminate your treasure with sin, filthy living, vile communication and disloyalty. Make your treasure desirable for your children and your children's children. Make sure your friends and neighbors walk away wanting what you have! Pass this treasure along to every person you know, churched or un-churched, saved or unsaved, Christian or not Christian … not the book, the treasure!

Finally, if this book has helped you to uncover the wealth of Salvation, then by all means, pass it on. It has been dedicated to you, the reader and please know that your name will be added to my special prayer voice for having read it.

Be blessed,
The End

THANK YOU FOR YOUR PURCHASE!
As my personal gift and show of appreciation,
please enjoy
"Saved: My Story, My Experience"
A Spiritual Autobiography
It starts right now!

CHAPTER ONE
The Basics
(You know, the stuff they put in funeral program obituaries)

I was born June 2, 1963 to William Fenner and Mary E.
Johnson at the Brooklyn Jewish Hospital on Prospect Place
and Classon Avenue. I lived at 192 St. Marks Avenue. By
then I already had 5 siblings, William Dennis (Tucson),
Marion Yvonne, Anthony Michael, Denise Darcelle
(NeNe), and Linda Darcelle I was number 6 in the clan and
almost two years later Paulette Cookie became number 7. I
could probably tell you stories about each one of them but I
will let them tell their own stories.

The truth is; my *real* life began on June 25, 1975. It was
the day I got saved. Before that, my "norm" was my
"norm". Life in the late sixties and seventies consisted of
hot pants parties, penny parties and steamed crab eating
parties. We had a party for everything. Mom sold food
and drinks at the parties and the rent got paid. We played
Pitty-Pat and Spades. Tucson was the family D.J. – "D.J.
Tomorrow" was his name. I remember hearing, "Love is
the Message" mixed with "Co-co-Mo, Let's Get It, Get It
Togetha." I remember turn-tables and 45 records. I can
still smell the fried chicken and fried fish, corn bread and
spaghetti. Whatch-u-say!

I don't remember my father in those days although I know him now. I heard stories about him though. I heard stories about how he gambled and packed the money with tape around mom's waist and sent her home from the "crap game" with the cash. I heard that at times it was enough to pay the rent and buy nice clothes for everybody but other times he had lost it all.

Drugs were really big in the seventies. I remember some of my mom's friends being pretty tore-up at times. Mom was a real night owl, she worked as a barmaid during the nights and cooked food at the bar during the day. I remember she was a really good cook and people were always in our house. She fed everybody. She was doing her thing and taking care of all seven of us the best way she could. She was amazing and I thought she could do anything. I still do.

We all went to school, had an immaculately clean apartment and we ate dinner every night. My mother cooked us real food; smothered pork chops, fried chicken, meatballs with rice baked inside that we called "porcupine", macaroni n cheese, string beans with smoked meat and my all-time favorite, black-eyed peas and neck bones. Sometimes we spent the night with "Auntie Verdale" on Underhill Avenue because our school, P.S. 9 was right across the street. She was not our real aunt but she was my mother's best friend. She cooked food that my mother said was "not real food" though; Chef Boy-R-Dee, but we loved it and got in all types of trouble for eating at her house. She had two sets of twins that we refer to as our cousins to this day; Kevin and Karen and Angie and Anthony a.k.a, "Red". We left there smelling like V.O.5 hair-grease and Strawberry pop-tarts. Other times, when the landlord let the city shut off the lights or the water in our apartment building, we stayed down the block at 188 with "Miss White" whose house smelled like spray starch and cigarettes in the morning. She had an autistic son named Stanley and three other sons named Larry, Thomas and Ricky. No girls. They were our "village", not real close family but family for real.

It turned out that school-work came easy for me. I loved to read and I was pretty smart. I remember my grade school teacher once referred to me as, "a Trip". I had overheard her conversation with another teacher and I remember being very offended. I showed it. When she finally asked what was wrong with me, I told her that I had heard her call me a "Trip" and didn't know what she meant by it but it didn't sound good to me. She explained that, "a Trip" referred to someone who was in their own world, doing their own thing and using their own mind ... on a trip. She said it was not an insult but it still felt like one to me.

Later on in my life, I found out that perhaps I really was, "a Trip". When life in the seventies was too much for me; When mom was gone a lot; when Tucson beat up Anthony for wearing his shirt or Marion and Nene got to fighting about one thing or another ... or the landlord was pounding on the door or whatever, I'd find my way to a closet, go inside and lose myself in one of my books. I had read, "Mr. Potter's Penguins" until I felt like part of the family; Judy Blume's, "Dear God, it's Me Margaret" and Dr. Funk's, "Power with Words", were my escape from planet earth! A trip.

Just so you know, I'm not saying that we had all bad days, nobody does. We had a good life filled with fun and family. My mother was a jack of all trades and she was and is and amazing woman. She is my "Phoenix" because I've seen her rise out of the ashes of life with her seven children on her arms, none of which did any time in prison, became addicts or failures in life. To this day we are all doing well and prospering in life and family. But it would not be true transparency if I wrote a story of life without expressing the feelings around those times of uncertainty and fear. Please remember, this is not a story about my family; this is a story about me, and my perception of life as I developed from childhood to adulthood.

We moved from St. Marks Avenue to Green Avenue then to Franklin Avenue. By that time I was about 9 or 10 and life began to look really dreadful to me. I'd look out of the window early in the morning to see the Methadone addicts nodding all the way to the ground but getting back up every time. I'd seen swollen hands and swollen feet knowing they were shooting needles in them. The building was dirty and the people were on drugs. The apartment was too small for us, and of course my mother had to lie about how many children she had in order to get an apartment so she told the landlord that I was a visiting relative from down south somewhere because there were too many of us for a three or even four bedroom apartment. It was easy enough to pull-off because I was, as they referred to me then, "high yellow" and everybody else was brown skinned.

The next-door neighbor was an old lady named Ms. Bey. Somehow, I became friends with her. I'd go next door to her house and listen to her tell me stories about when she was young and how her parents were share-croppers. I even went down south with her once and pulled potatoes out of the dirt, shucked corn and picked okra. I went fishing for the first time in my life and was scared to death when I caught a fish. I threw the fish and the rod into the water and was ready to go home. I decided that day that I hated the south and would never return.

It turned out that Ms. Bey was a palm-reader and fortune-teller. In the seventies, everybody had a hustle.

By the time I was about 12, we had moved again to 1025 Lenox Road. This address is the most significant for me. It was in the backyard of 1025 Lenox Road when my mother yelled to us from the window and asked if we wanted to go with her. In times past, that meant, to the bar and we'd sit on the high stools and have coke with real cherries inside, but not this time.

I knew immediately by the way she was dressed that we were not going to any bar. That night we were going to church. The last recollections I had of church were only two instances when I walked into a church by myself out of curiosity. Once on Green Avenue, I walked into a little church during the summer time. I sat inside and joined in with a youth group and the lady taught me the 23rd psalm. She told all of us to memorize it and come back the next day. It turned out that they had a vacation Bible camp going on. I memorized the 23rd psalm but I never went back to that church. We had neighbors who went to church and we could hear them singing and having church in their apartment. I remember wearing a white dress, white shoes and pressed hair to my grandmother's funeral. The other time was when we lived on Franklin Avenue and Aunty Verdale lived on Dean Street and Nostrand Avenue. I walked down to Bedford Central Presbyterian Church and wandered inside. I remember it being very, very different from the little church on Green Avenue; in fact, it was humongous. I remember that the priest was a white man and it was very quiet like a library. Nobody asked me anything and I just walked in and sat down on the bench. They passed a plate that had money in it and people were putting dollars and coins in but I had nothing to give. The experience was memorable because everything was so pretty and clean just like a museum. I never went back to that church either.

That night my mother took us to a little church where her
cousin, who she called, "Uncle Lawyer" was the pastor. It
was a week-night and they were having Bible Study. I met
his kids who were my cousins and they talked to me about
church. I remember them being shocked when I told them I
didn't go and had never really been to church. For them,
church was a part of their lives. It seemed they hated
church and couldn't wait to get grown and never come back
there. I was 12 years old and had no real church
experience. No Sunday-School. No Bible Study. No
Choir. No songs. No nothing, just the 23rd psalm. I was
happy to be there.

I had no idea that life for us was about to take a real turn. I
had no idea that the same night my mother had been
watching television and saw a white preacher named Billy
Graham say something like, "Give Christ your life today.
This may be your last chance". I had no idea that she had
taken seriously some words that I hadn't even remembered
saying to her before, "Mommy. What will happen to us
when you die?" She was on the path to recovery and knew
just how to get there.

Well, Uncle Lawyer was coming to get us for church on
Sunday. He had given her money to buy us all new dresses
and suits for my brothers. It was Sunday, June 25th and we
were going to church; I remember the date because it was
my friend Susan's birthday that day, her real name was
Beryl.

The chairs were covered with white pillow-cases and the
ladies had on funny looking hats. Everybody was dressed
up like church people. They sang songs that I did not
know. They all clapped on beat and made music with
tambourines and washing boards. The bent up hanger was

the scratcher. There was a drum set with only one or two pieces and a lady with a small afro played them. *"Do Lord, do Lord, Lord remember me, oh, Do Lord, do Lord, Lord remember me, Do Lord, do Lord, Lord remember me, oh, oh do Lord remember me."* It was simple enough. I got it. They would change the beginning and the rest was the same; "While I'm down here praying Lord, Lord remember me, oh, while I'm down here praying Lord, Lord remember me" etc. I remember feeling like it was so easy to be a part of this. I loved it.

When, "Uncle Lawyer" (Pastor Lawyer Carter) got up to preach, he stuttered a little and smiled a lot. I remember him saying that being saved was a good life. It was the first time I had ever heard the term, "saved". He said, "It's a simple, clean, holy life" and he had the warmest smile on his face and I really believed him. My life was not simple. My life was not clean and holy. I had to read books to escape what was going on in my head-my world. I didn't like my world. I often dreamt of murder. I wanted to kill the people who gave my mother pills. I wanted to kill all of my mother's friends. I didn't like them because they were drunk or high all the time. Some of them had puffy hands. I didn't like any of her boyfriends. I didn't want them to touch me or look at me. I felt like a misfit in my own family because I looked different from everybody and wasn't sure who our father was. I was suicidal. I swallowed a handful of my sister's Phenobarbitals and wanted to remove myself from my world and nobody knew that but me. It seemed like, "Uncle Lawyer" knew. He kept on saying it over and over, "It's a simple, clean, holy life."

While he was talking I tugged my mother's sleeve and asked her, "How do I get saved?" and right there she told me, "You have to tell God you are sorry for your sins and when Uncle Lawyer finishes, go up there and say you want to be saved." The first time I ever prayed in my life was right then. I closed my eyes and said, "Dear God, It's me Cynthia. (I had learned that from Judy Blume) I'm sorry for my sins." I could hardly wait until he finished preaching and I ran up to the front of the little church and said, "Hi Uncle Lawyer, I want to be saved please." He smiled and repeated, then yelled "Halleluhyun! The heavens are rejoicing because this young precious soul wants to give her life to Christ." I repeated words like this after him, "Lord Jesus, I repent for my sins. I'm sorry for whatever I have done wrong. I believe that you died for me and I believe that you love me. Please come into my heart and save me." and he said, "It's just that simple, sister Cynthinny, you are saved."

I can't say that I didn't feel different. I felt like something had really just happened even though I didn't see anything or really feel anything. I felt like my life was about to be better. I felt relieved as if a boulder was taken off of my shoulders and I would be able to live now. I believed him. I did not know then but I know now that I had *faith*.

After church everybody was talking to me. They were making a big deal out of what I had done. I remember the Elder, another cousin, said, "Don't stop now. You gotta get the Holy Ghost." She was short and hefty, older than my mother, I think, and had a lot of kids and grandkids I had no idea what she was talking about but if she said I needed it, I believed her and I wanted it. I could not wait until the next service.

We went back on Tuesday night and when we got there they were praying and I heard the lady who played the drums speaking another language. She was on her knees near the old broken piano, clapping and sweating and speaking another language. While I was on my knees I

asked one of my younger cousins what she was doing and
what language she was speaking. She whispered, "Oh that's
called tongues. You talk like that then you get the Holy
Ghost." I said, "So she's getting the Holy Ghost right
now?" she waived her hand, chuckled and said, "oh her,
she always gets the Holy Ghost." I was confused.

I was so excited. I needed to learn so much. I listened
carefully to everything the pastor said from the Bible but
that night he didn't say anything about speaking with
tongues or getting the Holy Ghost. After church I asked the
drum-lady about the Holy Ghost since she was always
getting it. She said you have to tarry for the Holy Ghost
and you'll get it. People just talked to you like you already
knew what this stuff meant. Sheesh, for me, everything
was new. All I knew about the word tarry was that Friday
night's services were called "Tarry services" and I planned
to be there on Friday.

I went home and looked up the word, *tarry* in the dictionary
to find that it meant, "wait" or "linger", like hang around. I
figured we would just go to church and wait around for the
Holy Ghost to come and then *get it* some kind of way and it
would make us speak in tongues.

When I went to school the next day, I was so mad because
all I had were pants to wear. The Elder had already told me
that saved girls didn't wear pants. It dawned on me that I
had a friend in my class who used to sing "church" songs
all the time. She wore pants all the time but I decided to
ask her if she was saved. To my surprise she was! She was
so happy to hear that I had gotten saved. She told me that
her grandfather was the Pastor of St. Mary's church on
Fulton Street and her whole family went there. She was
saved and so normal. I never knew – I guess I wouldn't
have known still, if I weren't saved myself.

We were in the 7th grade and she was very popular. She wore really nice clothes and had a nice shape so all the guys were after her. I wanted to be like her. It was like having the best of both worlds. She wore pants and never talked to them about the Bible and was just normal and she had the guys eating out of her hands.

Although she was very encouraging to me and very helpful in explaining things like the inner filling of the Holy Spirit, my desire to be attractive and popular like her proved to be a distraction to my salvation. I didn't want to fake it. I believed every single word of the Bible and every single word of my pastor and church leaders. I felt guilty wearing sexy pants to school once I discovered that I had hips. If you wear your panties tight enough your hips would show through your tight pants. I even had a few back-staircase encounters that I was not so proud of. I was overwhelmed with guilt and felt terrible but I didn't feel comfortable telling her about it because she was so happy. I realized then that there were different levels of commitment between saved people. All churches did not teach the same thing and all saved people did not live the same lifestyle. I started to notice the many different denominations and strange words on the church signs. It was not until then that I even took notice that my church had those, "extra words" too.

Prince of Peace Pentecostal Holiness Church, Inc. was the full name of my church and my mother's cousin, Elder Lawyer Carter was the Pastor. I began to ask so many questions that I was driving people crazy. It was so shocking that people would be so committed to a church and could not even explain what the words meant that were in the church name. I'm not saying they didn't know, I'm saying I couldn't get a straight, consistent answer between two people. I got so many different answers to the same question that I decided to try to find those words in the Bible for myself. It was impossible; first off, I didn't even have a Bible and second I had heard that it contained 66 different books! It would take me years to read all of them. I realized that salvation would take time, probably a lifetime to understand it all.

As a student in Junior High School, I was focused and serious about my grades. I worked hard and studied and came out on top every time. I vowed to be as committed to my Bible studies as I had been with my school-work. I attended Sunday-School and Bible Study without fail. If my mother was not going, I got on the number 7 bus, transferred to the 15 and went by myself. I was learning the Bible and getting to know God. I read the New Testament Gospels over and over and got to know what Jesus was like. It was like I was one of His disciples, following him around and repeating whatever he had said. I was a groupie.

For the first time in my life, our house was at peace. Mom was working and living right. We had taken on a new lease on life and things were going well. The sun was really shining and I had hope for the future. Life was good and I knew it was because of Jesus. The day my mom called us out of the backyard was the day our real life began.

CHAPTER TWO
Sister Cynthinny

Things progressed quickly for me. I was the Holiness Church's little wonder. I sure didn't mean to be but I say that because I was the only member my age that was serious about being saved. It seemed like my cousins were just there. They sang in the choir, ushered on the board, came to every service but couldn't wait to leave. I was involved in everything and got a lot of unwanted attention. Parents began to use me as the example to their kids, "you need to be saved like Sister Cynthinny" but these were my only friends. I felt like they hated my guts. They left me by myself, and when I showed up the conversations hushed. I developed the new nick-name, "Miss Missionary". My sisters didn't spare me either, I was "Miss Missionary" at home too. In hindsight I can admit that I was quite the self-righteous one. In the Holiness church you were taught that it was holiness or hell – no in-betweens; so I thought I was going to heaven and everybody that was not living right was going to hell. I felt compelled to get them saved. That didn't work.

By the time I was 14 they actually made me a real Missionary, gave me a license and everything. I was able to "speak" on what they called "platform" services. Those were services that had several speakers with time limited segments and specific subjects to speak about. Once they had a service and the subjects were, Saved, Sanctified and filled with the Holy Ghost. I chose to speak about the Holy Ghost. I had been to Tarry service after Tarry service. I said "Jesus, Jesus, Jesus" until my mouth got tired and my body was worn out, each time, they would say, "Keep on tarrying daughter He's right in your mouth. You'll get it soon." With the same breath, they would say, "The Holy Ghost is a gift. It comes on a glad heart and a sanctified life."

Well, I thought I *was* sanctified. I even stopped hanging around with my friend at school and the boys. I tried not to fuss and argue with my sisters and I refused to wear a pair of pants, not even in the dead cold winter. Getting the Holy Ghost was hard work but I was determined to get it because the Elder told me I needed it.

I did my studies on the inner-filling of the Holy Ghost and then I knew why I needed it. Acts 1:8 says *"But ye shall receive power, after that the Holy Ghost is come upon you: and ye shall be witnesses unto me both in Jerusalem, and in all Judea, and in Samaria, and unto the uttermost part of the earth."* Power! Wow. I wanted to have power to witness. I was scared to talk to anybody at school about Jesus and I didn't want to be scared to tell people about Jesus anymore. Now I *knew* I needed to get the Holy Ghost and I knew *why.*

After yet another long tarry service, and peaking around only to see the Elder dozing off to sleep during prayer and others repeating routinely saying, "Thank you Jesus, Thank you Jesus, Hallelujah", I was tired and bored. Still, the same thing, "Just keep on praying daughter you'll get it." I was done.

Thank God for Sunday because that afternoon, it was a big occasion of some sort and we had a guest speaker. Maybe it was the church anniversary because everybody in my family was there. They didn't usually stay for afternoon services. It was my first time seeing this preacher. He was short and had a rolling amplifier and a microphone. (Our church didn't use microphones; our voices were loud enough; At least that's what they said.) To my delight, he was preaching about the Holy Ghost. He was really good and at the end he said, "Some of y'all been tarryin' and tarryin' trying to get a free gift! Why would God make you work for something He's giving away for free? All you need to do is believe and you will receive." He asked, "Is there anybody here who wants to receive the Holy Ghost right now? If so, come up here." Without looking around at the pastor or the Elder for permission, I ran right up to that altar. It was a few of us up there and he walked over to each of us and asked, "Do you believe?" Before I could get the word, "yes" out of my mouth he had laid his hands on me and said, "Receive!" I need to take my time and tell you what happened next. I remember it like it was yesterday.

My body became very hot from my head to my toes. I started praising God and thanking Jesus. The more I clapped my hands the hotter I got. I felt something inside of me like a glowing fire. Not like fire that burns you but fire that warms you. Then when I closed my eyes I saw a vision of dark brown, like bronze feet in sandals and a white robe. Then I saw the same colored hands. In them was a white, pearl colored, glowing vase. The hands began to pour and this thick, shiny, white creamy substance came out and poured down on me. The next thing I remember was the little man with the microphone to my mouth and I heard myself speaking another language. I had no control over it.

62

I had received the gift of the Holy Ghost. The power of God had taken over my body and my mouth. I didn't know how to fake – nobody taught me so I knew it was real. I had not seen this man before then or since then, at least I didn't know if I did but I was so grateful because he made sense of what I had been hearing about the free gift of God. All the way home, I was shaking inside and felt like a drunk. I was weary but rejoicing inside, still speaking a language I did not know. I remember my sister Linda said, "Mommy, Cynthia is speaking Spanish".

That was on Sunday night. On some Monday nights they had a service that went around to different churches called, the Monday Night Fellowship. I remember being so excited to testify - stand up and talk - saying I had received the Holy Ghost. The service was at a church on Waverly and Atlantic Avenues. Up a flight of stairs and the pastor was a lady named Pastor Whittaker. That night Pastor Josephine Batts was the preacher. I didn't know her but I heard some people call her, "The Whip."

Well, I came up the stairs as happy as I could be but I noticed that the Elder from my church had her arms folded and was looking at me like I had done something wrong but I couldn't figure that out. As soon as I could, I got up and testified. "Giving honor to God. I want to thank God that yesterday I received the Holy Ghost!" People started saying, "Praise the Lord! Hallelujah. Yessuh!" It lasted just a few moments and died down. Right after that, the staring Elder got up to testify. She said, "Ah hah. I remember when I thought I had the Holy Ghost but

I didn't cuz I didn't get it like the Bible say. Can't
no man just *give* you the Holy Ghost. The Bible
Say, tarry til you be endewed with the Holy Ghost."
The people said "Amen" and I was crushed. Why
would she do that to me? What had I done wrong?
How could I be right and she be right too? Did I
really have the Holy Ghost? I was 14 years old and
a woman at least four times my age, an Elder in the
church had just said I did not have the Holy Ghost.
I was there. I had an experience. I believed. I
was crushed.

Not long after that, the preacher, "the Whip", got up
to preach. It was obvious that she didn't like what
had just happened. She went-in on the personal
nature of salvation and how no one can dictate how
God moves. She said, we don't have a monopoly
on God! He moves however he wants to move.
Only an individual who had received the Holy
Ghost can possibly know if they had received Him.
I got it. I understood that. I agreed with her
because I knew it. I had no doubt.

It turned out that there was this dictatorship in some
of the churches like mine that said, "if you don't do
things our way it is not right, it's not like the "Bible
say." It appeared to me that since that Elder didn't
approve of the way the visiting preacher operated,
she was accusing him of being out of the will of
God. The fact that he clearly said, "Only those that
were in the upper room had to tarry for the Holy
Ghost and once it came on the day of Pentecost, it
was just a matter of believing after that", would
have meant nothing to her.

The reason this was so devastating to me was because I loved her so much. I respected her and tried to do everything she said to do. Outside of church she was so nice. I just couldn't figure that out.

It was after that, that I realized, everybody in the Holiness church was not so holy. Some people were just down-right mean. Although the Elder was pretty nice to us most of the time, when it came to things like that, she was very stern but to me it felt very mean. When it came to the Scriptures, she would argue with the Pastor and he was like putty in her hands. She and my mother didn't hit it off either. They would argue and almost come to blows after church. They were family but this was church for God's sake!

There would be church meetings where they would argue back and forth. I remember one meeting where the Elder had told Pastor Carter something about my mother and they were going back and forth like enemies and my mother went stomping out toward the door. Pastor Carter yelled, "You better be careful walking out of here like that, God will kill you dead!" My mother kept walking and calling for my sister and me to come on. I was so scared, I thought God was really going to kill my mother dead.

Needless to say, God did not kill her. She is still alive and well today but that was quite scary. I told you before that I believed every single word that my Pastor had said, well, not any more after that. My mother's attendance began to dwindle after that and

I had started to see signs of her old life creeping in but I was focused and still did not miss a service.

We continued to go to Prince of Peace Pentecostal Holiness Church but I could see that our days there were numbered. More meetings, more fights, more threats and more arguments. After a while it seemed like everybody in the little church was angry about something, except the pastor; he continued to be the sweet, smiling man who said, "Salvation is just a sweet, clean, holy life." I wondered often if he had heard them throwing off on each other in testimony service or talking about each other after church. It became so regular that I simply got used to it and got an in-your-face revelation that holiness was much more than a word on a sign; these people were from the Holiness church but very few of them seemed to be holy. One of the regular congregational songs was, "To be like Jesus, to be like Jesus, how I long to be like him; so meek and lowly, so humble and holy, how I long to be like him." The more I read the four Gospels, the more I knew that these people were so, not like Jesus; only the pastor and others I did not know even came close.

I tried and tried to be like Jesus but the vision of Jesus would get so lost in the business of church that it became very difficult. I remember seriously asking God if this was the way he wanted things to be because most of it seemed much more like people than God, but I still tried.

Well, it was time for Holy Convocation; which, to me, meant we got on a bus and went to Virginia and did the same thing we did in Brooklyn, except there would be more people that we didn't know. The chatter about Convocation was all in the pews for weeks, "You going to Convocation? You know you gotta pay your dues? You bringing the kids?"

The trip started really early in the morning when it was still kind of dark outside. We would all meet at the church with a bunch of make-shift luggage, shopping bags and even a few garbage bags. Women wore head scarfs and "ride-the-bus" clothes. A hot mess! People had coolers filled with Kool-Aid, water and little squeezer quarter-waters. Royal Farms plastic bags with enough aluminum foil to wrap the entire bus twice. Greasy fried chicken and loaves of wonder bread; bologna, spiced ham and cheese sandwiches with mayonnaise for days; a year's supply of no-name chips and path-mark brand cookies. I don't even remember if my mother was there or not. I was on the bus because that's where the church people were supposed to be and mom said I could go.

We were always waiting for the choir-lady. She wasn't ready when pastor got there with the church van to pick her up and she had the most kids. She was the devotional leader and the choir director. She would sing solos every Sunday looking away from the people but would bless the house. Her favorite song was, *"Lead me, guide me along the way. Lord if you lead me I will not stray, take me through , dah dah, dah dah, dah dah with thee, lead me, oh Lord lead me. "* I never did find out what she was saying on the, "dah-dah" part and I don't know if anyone else knew either. We did not own one hymn book so we learned by listening. We used to go to her apartment for choir rehearsal. We loved her so much and she taught us so many songs; our hit song was, "Take me Back," an Andre Crouch original.

The choir-lady and Pastor finally arrived and we were ready to go to Holy Convocation in Portsmouth, VA. There was singing, talking, laughing, chicken-passing and sleeping, mostly sleeping for what seemed like 100 hours in that bus. We approached the Chesapeake Bay Bridge and everybody got so excited. It was the longest bridge I had ever seen, in fact, it was the only bridge I had ever seen. We didn't have a car and we didn't go anywhere. I just wanted to get off of that bus. I was not having fun. Remember, "Miss Missionary", didn't have any friends.

We arrived at the house where we were staying. It was a nice country house that was very clean and looked like one I had seen on "Little House on the Prairie". I remember feeling and noticing a calmness and a peace there. The house belonged to Pastor Griffin who was a short stocky lady with a voice like a man. She showed us to our rooms and we settled in. A few of us stayed there, a few others had family in VA, others stayed at the Holiday Inn but we would all meet together for service the next day. For dinner, Pastor Griffin brought out a big bowl of white spaghetti and a bottle of ketchup and said, "Eat up children, we got church in the morning." No, for real.

Holy Convocation was held at a nice church in Virginia that had a different name in the front. There were about 6 different Prince of Peace churches gathered. Prince of Peace Brooklyn, that

was us, Prince of Peace Manhattan, Bishop Walker
(The choir-lady's brother, but she couldn't get to
Harlem for church every Sunday so she stayed in
the Brooklyn church), Prince of Peace Albany, NY,
and Unity Prince of Peace, Pastor Josephine Batts,
"The Whip" and of course, the Prince of Peace
churches of Virginia; Suffolk and Portsmouth.

It was exciting to meet all the saints from all over
the place but I was really excited to see Pastor Batts
again because she came to my rescue after the Elder
got me at the Monday Night fellowship! We were
all wearing convocation tags. We got programs and
everything. This was a big deal. It turned out that
Convocation time also meant elevation time. No
wonder everyone was on their best behaviors, even
the Elder was being nice. New licenses were being
distributed during the Holy Convocation. This is
how it worked: Lay-members (saved people with no
titles who could do things in church) could be made
Missionaries (that was the lowest title you could
have I think.) Men could become Deacons, but there
were never too many, if any, of them. The only
men were my pastor, Bishop Walker and sometimes
Brother Green, the piano player. There were a
couple of young guys but they were busy kissing
my cousins on the slick side in the back of the bus.
Missionaries became Ministers, Ministers became
Evangelists or Elders and Elders became Assistant
Pastors.

The service was underway and all of the important
people were finally seated after the big march. The
singing was better because they used the best of all
the churches. Sister Mary from Albany was a really
good piano player and Bishop Walker's church had

a real good singer. It was good church. I was so
happy that the preacher for that service was my
favorite, Pastor Batts. I loved my pastor because he
was so much like Jesus but his preaching was a little
repetitive and he very rarely preached. He had
always let the Elder preach or someone else, but
mostly the Elder. Pastor Batts had a way of making
the Bible seem real. Most of all, she explained
things as she went along. That helped me a lot
because most of the time, I was just going along
with the motions, I really didn't know why I didn't
wear pants or act like "the world" except because
that's what they told me was a sanctified life.
Pastor Batts knew the Bible. She had facts. She
was very confident and the people always shook
their heads like, 'wow", whenever she would
preach. I wanted to know the Bible like that. I
wanted so badly to understand what I was reading
in the Bible and she had my full attention. I noticed
that while she preached, The Elder sat with her arms
folded and it was obvious that she did not care for
Pastor Batts. I can't remember now what Pastor
Batts' subject was but I knew then that it made a
difference in me. I remember what it was about
though. It was about being a witness for Jesus and
not being afraid to tell somebody about Jesus. She
said, "If you are ashamed of Him, he will be
ashamed of you before His father." She said it was
our job as Believers to win souls for Jesus. She said
every soul won in the earth gave you a stone in your
crown in heaven. I remember that thus far I didn't
have any stones in my crown and I vowed to
witness for Jesus. I had received the Holy Ghost
and I knew I had power so I was not afraid any
more.

On the way home I was walking with Sister Mary's son, David. I didn't know his name then but they had just arrived that day and I found out that they would also be staying at Pastor Griffin's house. As we walked back together, I remembered the message so clearly and the first thing I asked him was if he was saved. He said no and I went to work on him. I would be a witness for Jesus. I was on a mission. I told him everything I could think of about Jesus and why he should be saved. By the time we got close to the house he had asked what he had to do to be saved. Right there on the porch, I said, "Repeat after me. Dear Jesus, I'm a sinner. I'm sorry for my sins. I believe you died for me and that you rose again from the dead and I want you to come into my heart and save me." He did it and it was done! He was saved. It worked. My witnessing worked that fast! I had a star in my crown! I remember until this day how he stood on the steps of that porch and cried. He immediately said to his mother and Pastor Griffin with tears in his eyes, "I'm saved. I just got saved. Cynthia helped me get saved." I was crying, he was crying and his mother was saying "hallelujah". Pastor Griffin said in her deep voice, "Sister Cynthia, God is gonna use you."

Pastor Griffin's words went straight through me. I wasn't sure if it was the deepness of her voice or if, in fact, this lady was packing real power. After she had spoken those few words to me, I remember feeling like what she said had already happened. The fact that she said my name correctly helped. I lay across the bed that night feeling the night breeze of the country, smelling grass and hearing crickets in a place of peace and I remember thinking, the

Holy Ghost is real. I did receive it because I was a witness tonight and it worked! Down south was not so bad when you had the Holy Ghost.

To this day, they tell me that David is a pastor in Albany, NY. As I write this, I plan to try to connect with him, just because. Most people went by first names or last names – not both, i.e. Sister Mary, so I don't even know his last name but I will find out.

When the Convocation was over, The Elder was now the Assistant Pastor and I went from being a Missionary to being an Aspiring Minister. Nobody told me that my pastor had recommended me for that but I was happy and excited. It meant two things, I had to have a trial sermon and I had to pay $5 minister's dues at the next Convocation.

Well, the night had come for me to do my trial sermon. The Bishop would be there and all the other leaders and they would determine whether I qualified for a Minister's license or not. It was not just me and it was pretty much a done deal. They were not really judging me, they trusted the recommendation of my pastor so it was more like an "initial" sermon but they called it a trial sermon. After school that day, I remember that my friend or my brother had a bike and they had let me ride but my long skirt kept getting stuck in the chain so I went upstairs and asked my mother to pin it for me. She said, "Cynthia, you don't ride a bike with a skirt on. Just put on some pants to ride the bike." I was so reluctant to put on the pants but I wanted to ride the bike so I put them on and rode and rode. Well, my cousin saw me riding the bike with the pants on and she told the Elder's daughter that *Miss*

Missionary was wearing pants. She told her mother and while I was at home getting dressed to go and present my trial sermon, the Elder called and she told me about myself. She said that when you think you're hiding, God always had someone who sees. She said you can't live a double life or straddle the fence. She said, "Cynthia you know we don't wear pants. You know better. How can you preach to the other kids and you don't live it yourself?"

I was a mess. I was angry and confused. I was guilt-ridden and sick to my stomach. I remember going into the bathroom and throwing up. I was so confused. I was crying so hard that my mother asked what was wrong. I told her what happened and told her what the Elder had said. I said that I could not preach any trial sermon because I was too guilty. My mother said, "Cynthia, she is not God. She shouldn't have said anything to you, plus I am the one who told you to put the pants on and I am your mother, not her." She called the pastor and he said, "You tell Cynthinny don't pay that nonsense no never mind. Put you on a dress and come on and preach the word tonight."

The service was at Unity Prince of Peace on Broadway. I remember crying all the way there. My eyes were red and my hands were shaking like a leaf. I threw up again and my mother patted me on the back, hugged me and told me I could do it. The church was so clean and pretty and bigger than ours. All of the New York churches were there and I was scared to death. I had one verse, Job 16:19 *"Also now, Behold, my witness is in heaven, and my record is on high"* My subject was: "My witness is in Heaven". I planned to talk about being a witness

73

for Jesus on the earth and that it would give you a witness in heaven. I can't tell you I remember what I said at all that night but I can tell you that by the time I finished, everybody including my Pastor, my mother and my favorite preacher, Pastor Batts was standing up, crying and praising God, even the Elder! I honestly don't know what happened or what I said. I remember feeling like I had electricity going through me and words were coming out of my mouth so fast that I didn't remember even thinking them. I learned later that it was the anointing that came from the power of the Holy Ghost.

CHAPTER THREE
Unity Prince of Peace

After so many battles between my mom and the Elder and so many other factors, my mother decided to move on and take us to join Unity Prince of Peace with Pastor Batts. I wasn't really sure how I felt about that but I thought if it meant my mother would start coming back to church regularly that was good enough for me. I loved to hear Pastor Batts preach but I knew I would miss the choir-lady, the choir and Pastor Carter.

It turned out that the move was the best thing that could have ever happened to me. My family came back to church, we were all in the choir and my mom was back in *full effect*. The church was great! Brother Green came by and played the piano and services were really good. The best thing was the preaching. Pastor Batts was the best! Not only at our church but I found out that people loved her preaching in a lot of other churches. She was very popular and I went with her everywhere she went. I was her shadow.

Every Wednesday night was Bible Study. I was ecstatic. I learned so much about the Bible and she kept telling us that the Bible is not just for learning, it's for living. She said you get more out of the Bible when you live it than when you just learn it. She taught the Old Testament just like the New Testament and it was so clear that a five year old could understand it. Even when she preached, she didn't let Brother Green play music behind her, she would say, "I'm not singing, I don't need any music."

One Wednesday night she taught a dynamic lesson about faith. It changed my life forever. She taught the principles of faith and made me believe that nothing was possible without it! She also taught that faith without works was dead. She said you have to put your faith to work or it's useless to you. I went home rehearsing, "faith without works is dead. Faith without works is dead". I went to sleep saying it.

When I woke up the next day, I said, "Today I'm gonna use my faith!" I went to school on a mission. We had gym and while I was changing in the locker room I remembered that after gym everybody bought a can of soda from the soda machine.

I did not ever have any money to buy soda but today I would use my faith! I waited until everyone left the locker room and I walked over to the soda machine repeating, "Faith without works is dead". I said, "Lord, today I'm gonna use my faith and when I touch the button for a Sunkist Orange soda, it's going to come down." I looked around, put my nervous hand on the button, closed my eyes and pressed! 2 seconds later an orange Sunkist soda came down. I stood there crying and saying, "It works. Having faith really works." The teacher came to see what I was crying about and I told her, "I used my faith and got this soda. Faith works." She smiled and told me to hurry on to class before the bell rang.

It meant very little if anything to her, and probably means very little to many, but it was life-changing for me. To this day I trust God for anything and my assignment to the body of Christ is to help Believers to Believe.

Over the years, Pastor Batts had *hand-fed* me the Bible. I learned so very much from her teaching. I learned the principles of salvation, sanctification and holy living. I learned about God and how to please him. I wanted to please him. I wanted him not just to love me but to like me. I wanted God to be proud to say that I was his daughter. Whenever Pastor Batts couldn't teach or was led of the Lord, she would let her brother-in-law teach, (Her sister's husband) Elder Dan Carter (who was also Pastor Lawyer Carter's older brother.) I have to tell you about him.

He was magnificent! He was funny and he really knew the Bible. He was a walking Bible with a miraculous testimony. My mom called him "Uncle Dan" like "Uncle Lawyer". He testified about being in the "mently institution" all of his life. He would say, "I was crazy!" He said he had seen Pastor Batts' sister Bertha working or visiting at the hospital and God told him she would be his wife. He said he would ask God how he could get a wife and he was "mently" and didn't even know how to read. He said he was 16 or 19 years old in the 4th grade down south because he couldn't learn. He said God said he was going to teach him how to read. He said Bertha gave him a Bible and God taught him how to read it. The more he read the Bible, the better he became. He said whenever he would read the Bible he would feel the power of God. God taught him how to read and healed his mind. He eventually married Bertha Batts and became a prolific Bible teacher. He out-lived

Bertha and tended to her during a long bout with cancer. I spent hours a day at their apartment and watched him patiently care for his dying wife while so often she would become angry and mean, throwing things at him. Whenever she would finally go to sleep, he would sit down and teach me the Bible. He loved it. It was all he ever talked about. He never once complained about his wife. He loved her and cared for her until the day she died.

He lived alone and took care of himself without a home attendant for years after that, teaching and preaching pure Bible truth and telling funny jokes. The day he died, he called his God-daughter, who was a member of our church but often went by to help him out after his wife died. He told her to get his brown suit out of the closet for him. He only had two suits, a black one and a brown one. He wore the black one during the week and the brown one on Sundays. Since it was only Tuesday, she told him he was getting senile because he always wore his black suit to Bible Study on Tuesdays. He said, "Naw. Just do like I tell you. I want to wear my good suit today because I'm going away." He insisted and she was convinced that the old man had gone senile. When he didn't come to church that night, the saints went to his house to find him seated in the chair, fully dressed in his brown suit, brown hat with his Bible in his lap. He had passed from death unto life and looked peacefully asleep.

These are my real experiences. These are things I actually lived and saw. Nobody told me these stories except the people who were actually there and had no reason to make things up. To this day, when I pray, I thank God for those he had placed in my life, the late Pastor Carter, Uncle Dan, Pastor Griffin, Elder Peebles; and Sister Ruth who is still a member of Prince of Peace Holiness church today, but most of all, my pastor, my mentor Josephine Batts.

CHAPTER FOUR
Pastor Josephine Batts

As the years went by, I had become so close to
Pastor Batts that people actually thought I was her
daughter. I even looked a little like her niece
Carolyn who was her older Sister, Pearl's daughter.

Pastor Batts was the youngest of seven. She had
five sisters and one brother. All of her sisters
attended her church, some more often than others
and her brother was the pastor of The Free Gift
Baptist Church in Brooklyn. I did not know him
and only learned of him at his funeral. The three
sisters who were mostly at the church were, Mary
Overton, Pearl and Clara. Bertha was an Evangelist
and was gone a lot until she got sick and died. The
oldest one, "Beckka" was a little eccentric I think.
She showed up and disappeared, babbling about
things I could never understand, but she smiled a
lot.

Mother Overton was the closest one to Pastor Batts,
they actually lived in the same house on Sterling
Place in Brooklyn. She, Elder Delores Smith and
Pastor Batts were inseparable and they ran the
church. Mother Overton made all of her clothes and
she taught me how to sew. I made skirts and
pillows and easy-sew patterns from Simplicity.

I spent a lot of time at their house. The same peace
I felt at Pastor Griffin's house was also in theirs.
My house was loud and busy. My brother played
music, my sisters went out to parties and
periodically my mother was back in the world. She

80

was in and out of the church but she always loved God and always kept us focused on Jesus. When she was good she was very good but when she was bad – woe unto to those who got crossed in her path. I realize now that it may have been easier for me to stay out of the world because I was never really in the world. I got saved at a young age and my temptations were minimal compared to my mom's.

After church some nights I would go home with Pastor Batts and we would eat Corn Flakes and talk about the Bible. When I knew it was getting late, I would tell her how peaceful it was at her house and she would say, "Sister Cynthia, I have a deep-settled peace within my gates that the world cannot disturb." She said that often and I quote it as my life's goal to this day. I will talk more about the importance of peace in my life later on, I promise.

I should mention that by that time we had moved to 239 New York Avenue between St. John's and Sterling Places and Pastor Batts lived on Sterling Place between Brooklyn and Kingston, just around the corner. Often, when I'd come home my mother was angry, I know now that she was very concerned about losing influence over her children. She had been very protective of us all of our lives. She raised us single-handedly with the help of God and would not let anyone else take that credit away from her. It seemed that I had replaced her with Pastor Batts. I never felt like that. I loved my mother to the depths and would even die for her no matter what. She was my mother and Pastor Batts was my Pastor, but I think my actions caused my mom to

see things differently and she seemed determined to
control the situation.

I came home one night as happy as I could be and
Mom went off. Did I think Pastor Batts was better
than her? She seemed determined to paint the Pastor
in the darkest light possible so that I could see that
she wasn't so holy and she wasn't better than her.
Before you judge my mother too harshly, consider
that she had struggled and worked really hard to
raise her seven children alone and she wanted to be
our hero. She was misguided in her thoughts that
anyone could ever replace her to us. She had her
reasons but from where I was looking she was
insecure and jealous for no real reason. I thought
she was tormented by thoughts of betrayal and
abandonment by her children, we were all she had.

Pastor Batts had never once tried to replace her.
She prayed for her all the time and encouraged me
to pray for her. She loved my mother dearly. Well.
That night I argued with my mother about trying to
make me choose between them, I did not
understand and I was very angry. I was raging and
being disrespectful so my mother told me to get out
of her house and go and see if Pastor Batts would
let me live with her. She said, you'll see, she's
gonna send your little yellow behind right back over
here with me. You'll see how holy your little angel
is then. I was furious. I slammed the door and
headed back to Sterling place. I just knew Pastor
Batts would take me in and rescue me from the
chaos! Well, she smiled and chuckled with her
usual peaceful demeanor. She listened to me
ranting and raving and let me calm down and kindly
told me I could not stay there with her. I had to go
back home with my mother. I was embarrassed and

82

I was emotional and what my mother said had taken root as a seed in my spirit. That night, for the first time in my life, I felt that maybe Pastor Batts was not that holy vessel that I had believed she was and it was all because I could not get my way.

I went back home, humbled with my tail between my legs and had to beg my mother to forgive me. By that time she wasn't even angry anymore. She hugged me and kissed me and sent me to bed but when I got in the bed I could not sleep. Everything she had said about the pastor while she was angry was on repeat in my head. I started questioning Pastor's relationship with Elder Delores Smith who had left her husband and family to live with Pastor Batts. The seeds were sown. I questioned whether they lied to the lawyer about a car accident they had while my sister Linda was in the car with them. My mother said they were trying to beat Linda out of her money. I started hearing the voices of her own sister Pearl Batts who would whisper that she was a dictator while we were kneeling down to pray. I heard the Elder and Bishop Carter's voices in my head repeating negativity about the lady I had held so dearly. Darkness was over-taking me and I just wanted it to end. How could she not be who I thought she was? How can she be so influential over my life and be a fake? Was any of this holiness business real? I remember the anger. I remember the confusion. I remember the pain. I didn't know then but I know now that the devil had won a major victory that night but it didn't start that night, it started with the seeds of negative words and gossip from people all around me and hit the bulls-eye when I could not have my way.

By then I was about 18 and my faith was shattered.
I made it through High School as a saved young
lady. I worked in Mays after school – keeping busy
helped me stay focused. It helped me to stay saved.
The days rolled into one another, I was lost and
confused. I remember thinking that I had given my
whole life to this and it was all a fake. I went to
church but had the idea that it was all fake, but I
would get down on my knees to pray and the peace
of God would overtake me, the power of God would
move on me and I would get up again refreshed and
revived but still so very confused.

I wanted to walk away but I was compelled to stay.
I went with the motions knowing all along that
Pastor Batts knew. She knew and instead of
fighting back, she would cry in prayer. She never
retaliated. She never offered a defense for herself. I
could not even repeat to her the words that I had
heard said about her but she knew. She would pat
me on the back and say, "Sister Cynthia, I'm
praying for you baby."

I watched her in prayer. I watched her go from the
strong, confident figure who stood tall before us to a
humble, seemingly weak, slumped over figure
immersed in tears. She would pray and clap her
hands in between sentences, I saw her get
strengthened in prayer and stand up again with
confidence and revelation, time after time.

Things didn't get better from there. It turned out,
through rumors, that the city had offered her money
for our church on Broadway. They say she sold the
building to buy a house for herself in Virginia.
Most of the rumors came from her sisters. We

moved to a small raggedy rented store-front on Ralph Avenue with no explanation. I didn't care. I was angry. She was planning to leave us. It looked like she was going to just take the money and run. Her sister had already moved to Virginia – Mother Overton left. Elder Delores Smith had died from the injury sustained in the car accident that she, Pastor Batts and my sister Linda were involved in. We prayed for her recovery and she still died. The rumors were incessant and I believed that if the rumors were not true, she would have recovered. Another member suddenly discovered a brain tumor and died. Things were just getting worse and my faith couldn't cut it. To make matters worse, the announcement came; Pastor Batts was indeed leaving to go to Virginia! Once she said it, I stopped listening. My heart was hardened and I was very angry. I felt abandoned and deceived. It was the last day I had ever walked into that church.

I went home in the middle of the day on a Sunday afternoon. I went straight into my room and cried myself sick. Angry crying is hard on the body. The days and weeks to follow were a fog to me. I did not call. I did not go. I did not communicate. I was a mess. I did not attend church – that was killing me. I considered some of the other churches we had fellowship with but they were all the same … fake. I was in a bad place with no idea how to get out. I was also a preacher. I did not show up for my engagements. I did not call. I just did nothing.

My soul longed for God. My soul needed fellowship with God. I could not backslide. I could not get away from God. His presence was deeply rooted inside of me. I had received the inner-filling of the Holy Spirit for real and I could not rest. I was angry but my soul wanted God. I was hurting in a place I could not describe but I still longed for God.

CHAPTER FIVE
The She-Eagle Stirreth – Brooklyn Tabernacle

One Friday night I just started walking down
Nostrand Avenue, not knowing where in the world I
was going. It was Friday night; I had been in prayer
every Friday night for years but I could not go back.
I just walked and walked. I started out at St. Johns
and Nostrand and walked. By the time I got to
Lexington Avenue I started to see people dressed
like church. I saw prayer caps, white dresses, dark
suits and Bibles going toward Lafayette Avenue. I
followed them. They turned at Lafayette and went
into Brooklyn Tabernacle. I followed them inside.

The church was so big and the pulpit was on the
floor while the seats were high up in a circle. It was
nice and beautiful inside but I was a stranger. I had
never been in a church like this one but the people
looked the same as they did in my church. No
make-up. No pants. Prayer-caps and long skirts. It
was a "big, little-church" if you get that.

I walked inside, following the crowd of people
while avoiding eye-contact. I found a seat way up
top and deeply in the middle. The Praise team was
singing, the music was wonderful and the
atmosphere was charged. When the music faded, a
group of mothers, dressed like catholic nuns walked
slowly in a line to the front row seats. Behind them
were men dressed in suits, mostly black. They were
the Ministers and the last one was the Pastor, Dr.
C.R. Johnson. He had the most electric and
warming smile. He shook hands and smiled,
waving at the congregation all the way to his seat.

I was a mess. I was so confused and so sad. I had no idea why I was in this church. I did not know one person there but I did not leave.

Pastor Johnson began to preach from Deuteronomy 32:11 – The She-eagle stirreth her nest…. His subject was, "Rejuvenaton: The Eagle Stirreth her nest". It would prove to be the most prolific evidence to me that God was real and that He really had of way of reaching his people. I was important to God. He had indeed led me to that church that night. The pastor described the plight of the eagle that had lost his way. The she-eagle whose nature is swift and keen and very rarely, if ever, misses its prey had become weak and her eyes were dim. She swooped down for her prey and missed it. She tried again and again and missed it. I was the she-eagle that had lost her way. I was weak and defeated, lost and could not find my way.

He went on further to say that the she-eagle turned her nose upward and soared to the top of a high mountain, moved her self over to a big sharp rock where she began to beat her wings upon it. Over and over, she'd beat that wing upon the rock until dead weights and useless feathers began to fall off. The eagle would rejuvenate herself. Although it was painful, the pain was necessary for her survival.

I was convinced without a shadow of doubt that the message was directly intended for me. I was the she-eagle! I was dying spiritually. I had missed my mark! I felt the anointing and the power of God consume me. While he was speaking I became overwhelmed. I felt the same warmth of the Holy Spirit that I had felt as a child. I was being rejuvenated by the Word of God. This is the best that I can do to explain what happened to me that night. I was obviously very much noticed; the pastor looked directly at me and pointed at me and said, "Stir your nest daughter, stir your nest and fly again." Of all the people assembled, he noticed me. Perhaps the congregation was so accustomed to his preaching that they were unresponsive. Perhaps I was really making a scene. I never stood up. I sat there and cried until my face was turning ruby red. I tried hard not to make a scene but I was being rejuvenated!

That night proved to me that I had purpose and that God thought I was special enough to send me an on-time, 9-1-1 emergency word. I had no idea what would be next for me but I knew it was in Him! I was back.

I started attending services there regularly. I never joined but I was committed to every service. Once the pastor pointed me out again and said, "Are you enjoying your new church daughter?" I looked around to see who he was talking to, and he assured me that he was talking to me. I nodded yes. He then asked me to stop in his office before I left. Although I quickly nodded, "O.K.", I was very nervous and almost reluctant. I didn't know him. I didn't know anyone and I didn't think I was ready to commit to joining the church for real. But I did go into his office.

There were several people in his office and he began to say that the Good-Friday service was approaching and he would have a service called, "The Seven Last Sayings of Jesus Christ". I knew it well. Each speaker would elaborate on one of the sayings. It was always a big deal. But I had no clue why I was there. He began to say, Minister so and so, I want you take the first one, Minister so and so, the second … I would just wait until this was over to see what he wanted with me. Then he said, Sister Johnson I would like for you to do word number four. I just knew he was talking to his wife, Ruby Johnson but she was not even in the room. He looked at me and said my whole name, "Cynthia Johnson" will do number four and he continued. I was stuck. Frozen in time. How did he even know my name? Who told him I was a preacher? I'm not doing this. I don't want to preach and I sure don't want to preach in this big church. I will wait until everyone left and tell him I'm not doing this.

Everyone accepted their assignment and began to leave the office. I waited. Then I said, "Pastor Johnson, I'm sorry but are you sure you want me to speak?" He smiled and said, "Yes. I'm led of the Lord to use you." I said, "but how do you know if I can do it and how do you know my name?" he chuckled and said, "Oh daughter, I've heard many good things about you." I was so confused. I was from a little holiness church with 8 members and had not been to church for months. Who could possibly tell this great man anything about me? It turned out that his musician used to play for a group called, the T.T.O.J, I had no idea what the acronym meant but he obviously told the pastor that I was a preacher and a pretty good one. His group used to sing at our little church choir anniversaries and he knew me but I didn't know him. I saw him in the musicians section but I never recognized him as anyone that I knew.

Well, I was still afraid and reluctant so when he said, "I just need you to wear black and white, take off your earrings and be here by 7 to march in with the ministers", I saw my way out! I asked why I had to take off my earrings. I didn't want to and I was never taught that anything was wrong with wearing earrings; pants, make-up, nail polish, yes, but not earrings! So, I thought that if I refused to take off my earrings, he would find someone else to do word number 4. He laughed and told me to take out the earrings and be there by 7 in black and white.

I was a nervous wreck every day leading up to that Friday night. The service night came and I was a wreck. I did look at the text but I was too nervous to get it together so I decided to show up late, in the earrings and get eliminated. It did not work. When I came in, the pastor scanned the crowd and found me. Pointed to me and gestured to me to come down. I pointed to my earrings and still he waived for me to come down. The usher came and escorted me to my spot in the chairs as the speaker for the fourth word.

I can't recall very much from there except I remember the warm feeling and the electricity running through my body as I talked about the fourth word; "Eli, Eli La Ma Sabachthani – My God, My God, Why hast thou forsaken me". My subject was, "The Ninth Hour Trade" – somehow I tried to portray how Jesus traded places with us at the ninth hour as he became sin for us and took the penalty of death for us. I can't recall all of the details but I remember the music behind me and I remember the people standing and yelling and shouting. I remember the dance that broke out after that. I remember the Mother's Board in a high praise. I remember that because they usually sat there like the Sanhedrin Court but this time they were dancing. They approved! I don't think the other speakers ever got to do their word and the last thing I remember was looking at Pastor Johnson and he was smiling with his thumb up.

The nights and the days, weeks and months to follow are all a fog. The people treated me like a celebrity and I was not sure what had happened. I don't remember half of what I'd said but I remember feeling the power of the Holy Spirit giving me words to say. It was God speaking life to His people through me. I was back – somewhere with no direction and no plans. I would let God guide my life.

The Brooklyn Tabernacle at 600 Lafayette Avenue was my home for that season although I never formally joined the church.

By then I was about 19 or 20 and had graduated from Canarsie High School, gotten a job at AT&T. I had applied for the job when I was in the tenth grade because they told me it took a long time to get hired at these places. My teacher and Guidance Counselor had encouraged all of the honor students to apply to all of the Fortune 500 companies in the tenth grade. In Junior High School I was selected to receive a full scholarship for High School and college through the ABC (A Better Chance) program for under-privileged honor students but it was either all the way in Japan or in Washington, D.C. both of which were too far for me to go to my church so I declined and went to Canarsie High School.

I had favor with God. The A T&T recruiter called my house the night of my graduation and offered me an interview. I got the job as a Representative at 18 years old with only a High School diploma. Most people started as an Operator and moved up to Representative and I was the youngest person there. It was a hostile environment for me but I went to work every day thanking God for favor.

I included that because I want you to see that when your life is in alignment with the Word of God, things happen in your favor. It had nothing to do with my GPA; nothing to do with anything that I had done except get saved!

While there, I enrolled in Long Island University because it was right next door to my job at 395 Flatbush Avenue. I worked during the day and went to classes at night. I then joined C.B.I – Community Bible Institute; so I worked 9-5, went to L.I.U from 6-10 but in-between 8:30-9:15 I went to C.B.I at 600 Lafayette Avenue for Bible School. I took only one class at a time and the first class I took was, "Faith" with Dr. Copeland, the Assistant Pastor of Brooklyn Tabernacle.

I chose the "Faith" class because I had faith. I believed everything the Bible said. I used my faith and it always worked. From the time I got the Sunkist orange soda to everything else that followed, I prayed to God and he supplied all of my needs. Period! The Faith class took my faith to another level. I learned the dynamics of faith and studied the heroes of faith. To this day my faith is focused and unshaken.

It was nearly a year before I began to lose enthusiasm at the church. It became a series of boring services, the pastor was always traveling to India and Pastor Copeland was filling in with the preaching. He was a great preacher but I still didn't fit in there. I felt the people were very self-righteous like I was when I was younger in the Holiness church. I was in the midst of a growing awareness and I wanted more. I was getting older and I didn't feel like I ever belonged there but I would not leave unless I honestly was led of the Lord. (Which meant, to me, that something would happen to make the move obvious; not just a feeling. Boredom was not a legitimate reason to leave a church.)

CHAPTER SIX
New Life Tabernacle

I still attended every service and took other classes at C.B.I. While sitting in a tent service, I noticed a long blue Cadillac that would pull up alongside the tent where the musicians sat. A few minutes later, the young musician that knew me from T.T.O.J days would leave and hop into the Cadillac and it pulled off. I began to notice that happening often so one day I asked him where he was going in that Cadillac. He explained to me that he was the musician for a preacher named Eric Figueroa and for his wife who used to sing before he preached.

One day I was sitting in the tent bored to death and I saw the Cadillac pull up so I slipped out of the tent and asked them if I could go. They were happy to have me. I squeezed in with the preacher, his wife, his secretary and the musician and we went to this church in Bedford Stuyvesant on Decatur Street in the middle of the block. I had never in my life heard singing like that! Doreen Figueroa wrecked the place! When Eric Figueroa started preaching the place was still a wreck from his wife's singing. He was great! He preached a powerful message and it just got worse. The people were going bananas and it was very exciting. I was glad they had let me tag along. Afterward I talked with the secretary, she said, "girl, it's always like this. They work as a team. She sings and he preaches and out the door we go to the next engagement!" She then said, "You should join his crusade team, it's fun." They dropped me off at home and it had been a great day.

I never considered joining any crusade team. I was already in college and Bible school with a full-time job! I continued going to Brooklyn Tabernacle for a few more months and one night the musician told me that the preacher, Figueroa was starting his own church and was looking for people to join the choir. It turned out that the church he was starting was only two blocks from my house! Immediately that felt like the kind of thing that made me think God was leading me. I knew I liked the way he preached and I knew I liked what I felt while his wife was singing but I didn't know about joining his church. I would do a drive-by. One Tuesday night I decided to walk over to the choir rehearsal just to see what they were about.

I went to 1476 Bedford Avenue at the corner of Sterling Place. It was a big building with all kinds of dragons across the top. The first floor lobby had statues of naked people. It looked more like a museum than a church. I heard the music from downstairs! It was awesome. I went up the stairs and sat in the back on the folding chairs. The people were dressed normally. Some of the ladies even wore pants! They had on Jeans and sneakers, sweat suits and work clothes.

I sat there about 10 minutes before the pastor told me to come up to the choir. Without asking me, he just told somebody to find out if I was alto or soprano. His wife came over and asked me to sing "Happy Birthday". Two seconds into the song she said, "We got another Soprano. Go over there to that section." I didn't want to be in the choir. I was only there to check them out but I didn't have much of a choice – they put me in the choir. It was all pretty new to me and pretty exciting, when I sang with the others I felt like I could sing!

After rehearsal was over, they were all preparing to start cleaning their new church. I was preparing to walk back home when the pastor called me out loud and asked me, "What church do you belong to?" Surprised, I said, "Well I go to Brooklyn Tabernacle but I never joined." He said, "We got a new member y'all! I was laughing and the few people there were clapping and saying, "Hallelujah." I thought, *Was he serious? You can't just make people join your church!*

His wife was so nice, she said, "Girl, that's how he is, but mind you, he always gets his way." She laughed and kept it moving. She said, "Our Pre-service is Sunday afternoon at 3 O'clock, you coming?" I figured, 3 O'clock is after the service at Brooklyn Tabernacle anyway so I said "yes." She said, "Good, we're wearing white."

The rest, as they say, is history. When I came into New Life Tabernacle the service was in full sway. The presence of God was over-whelming and I was swept away in the presence of God. For the first time in over a year, I danced. I danced and danced until I exhausted myself and the First Lady came and put her hand on my back. I felt the presence of a loving God through her touch and to this day it is the same. My burdens were lifted and I felt a release in my spirit. This is where I was supposed to be.

One night after choir rehearsal, I was surprised to see Pastor C.R. Johnson coming up the back staircase. He stood back there for a few moments.

I waved and smiled. It was awkward because I had never communicated with him about leaving. He was in India at the time plus I was not technically a member of his church. I was not sure why he was there but it did not feel good. When he was leaving he waived at Pastor Figueroa and said, "You'll do fine if you hold up a standard Pastor. Hold up a standard." Then he left.

It was then that the term "standard" turned-on my Holiness church conviction and it came upon me. I looked around at the women in pants and make-up, some of the guys were obviously gay, they joked all night long and it was just no *standard*. Although I felt the presence of God during the services and was sure that God had led me to this place, I began to feel so guilt-ridden. I became overwhelmed with guilt. I had not spoken a word to Pastor Batts in over a year. I was still angry with her for leaving but I felt so guilty. Had I become a defector of the faith? Had I let down the standard of the Holiness church? Am I feeling right in the wrong place? I was on my own making choices and decisions without counseling. I just went wherever I thought the spirit of the Lord was leading me but what if I was wrong?

I asked Pastor Figueroa if I could use the phone upstairs. I called my God-sister who used to go to Unity Prince of Peace. She gave me a number for Pastor Batts. I was shaking but I called anyway. When she answered, the peace I always felt around her was still there. My anxiety left and even though I was guilty and embarrassed, I felt like everything would be all right. I started talking and with a cracked voice and a face full of tears, I told her everything. I told her about the anger, the disappointment and the broken heart. She never interrupted me. I was rattling on. I then told her about Brooklyn Tabernacle and New Life Tabernacle. I told her what Pastor Johnson said. I let it all go.

Although she sounded very calm and chuckled her usual chuckle I knew that I had struck a nerve. I knew the move was as difficult for her as it was for me. I knew I had hurt her by leaving the way that I did. She had been given some misinformation by others about my state because to them I appeared to be a defector of the faith – a backslider who still liked church. I was far from it. I had been forced to have a personal relationship with God. I was all alone and had to learn his voice for myself. I thought I had it until that night.

I expected Pastor Batts to go in on the lack of a standard where I was but instead she said, "Sister Cynthia, we will all know in time, if this was the right move for you or not but I am praying for you as always." She sounded disappointed and sad but spoke her best truth to me at the time. To hear her say that she was praying for me, *as* always, gave me confidence to continue. I decided to let time tell.

I had joined New Life Tabernacle in August of 1983. I was the only female preacher there. I realized quickly that I was not the soloist that they celebrated in the Holiness church. I learned so much about God from Pastor Figueroa, I learned the freedom of the term "personal" in relationship with Christ. He was not a dictator and was very open-minded. He gave everybody the benefit of the doubt and taught me the power of loving people *on their level*. He often shared with me that it was not wise to try to take people where they were not ready to go or to limit your love only to people who met your standards. He taught and still preaches that we must love everyone right where they are.

It was a 15-year baptism for me, out of the traditional choke-hold of legalism into the bondage-free living of real relationship with Christ. To this day I appreciate his tutelage. He fathered me in the personal areas of my life, having grown up without a natural father in the home. He mentored me as a preacher and Evangelist and he maximized my quick wit and brought the funny into my life. I learned that it was not a sin to laugh. I didn't even know how bound I was until I got free. Does that make any sense?

It was at New Life Tabernacle that doors opened most for the ministry God had placed in me. I was every choir concert's M.C. I preached at platform services and alone, my pastor even let me preach in his place and on Sunday mornings at my church. He taught me the administrative business of ministry; he taught me the power and benefits of sowing seed and paying tithes. He stretched us to become faithful givers and supporters of the ministry and constantly reminded us that God would bless us if we learned to give.
Life at New Life Tabernacle was exciting and eventful. Never a dull moment. I met distinguished ministers, famous singers and political figures. Everyone knew Pastor Eric R. Figueroa, his wife Doreen Figueroa and subsequently everyone knew his Evangelist, Cynthia Johnson. I felt famous.

In those years I grew up for real. I suffered from my mistakes. It was during those years that learning to live without the safety of self-righteousness and legalism forced me to face real grown-up emotions. I had to make hard choices. Sometimes I passed sometimes I failed. I sinned and I repented. I fell and I got up. I got myself into all kinds of stupid messes but through it all, God was with me and he always brought me back. During the bad seasons, I pondered what Pastor Batts had said and thought, maybe time is telling me I made the wrong move but I think I was just growing older and becoming a woman. I continued to do what was right for me to do as a member of my church. Time was not over. Pastor Figueroa was right there to help me get out of whatever I had gotten my stupid self into but he never made me feel stupid. He did laugh at me. Oh yes, I was the butt of a few jokes – no one was safe but he ministered to me and got me back on straight street every time. Now that's all you're getting so don't expect details.

I actually grew up in New Life Tabernacle and they were my extended family. We laughed, we loved, we fought, we grew and we did all of that growing together. An invisible three-fold cord was developed and *stamped indelibly upon the retina of my mind* – (I got that from a snippet I heard of Pastor Devore Chapman a long time ago – I just never forgot it.)

In late 1990, after having been at New Life for some seven or so years, I was about 26 years old and every gentleman that came by to see me was a potential husband in their eyes. They were trying to marry me off! I used to say, "I wouldn't marry Adam and Eve Better not ask me." One day I was so frustrated by the constant teasing about who I would marry. I sat by my First Lady and said, "Sister Figueroa, you see these guys that come around her looking at me? I go out with them sometimes and I enjoy their company but the truth is, I don't feel anything for any of them. It seems they all have some kind of issue or they just irritate me. I'm starting to believe it might be me. I know I'm not into girls. I'm not crazy but these cats are losers." Well, she cracked up laughing and got really serious, patted me on my knee and said, "Cynty, things happen so quickly. When the right one shows up, you'll know it's him because you'll be willing to what you would not do, just for him." That was deep but it sure sounded real to me. At present, I wouldn't have walked an extra mile for any of those guys.

CHAPTER SEVEN
Me and Archie

It turned out that my First Lady was so right, things did happen quickly. Around November, 1990 I was asleep in the early evening because I was working the midnight shift at Dow Jones. My house phone rang and when I answered I heard this gentleman's deep voice on the line. "Hello, may I speak to Cynthia Johnson? My name is Archie McInnis but everybody calls me Bobby. My sisters say that I know you from Pastor Batts' church, do you remember me?" I admit, publicly and in print, I felt all *wooly* inside. Awww shoot! I did remember him. Although when we were younger I was so saved I couldn't admit that he was kind of cute, I was older now and apparently, so was he. My whole demeanor changed and I had a cheese grin all the way across my face. Without trying, I put on my, *"be cute"* voice and answered, "Yes. I remember you."

The conversation went on and he told me that he had gotten my number off of the back of our church program from Brother Charles Tillman who was a member of New Life Tabernacle and a fellow student with him in an E.M.T Training school. He was asking about our choir to see if he could get the choir to sing at his church's choir anniversary and Charles had directed him to me. When he got home I don't know if he told his sisters or if they saw the program, they said, "Cynthia Johnson? We know her and you do too!" His mother pulled out the photo albums and there I was in many pictures at their church singing with Pastor Batts' choir during their choir anniversary. The little churches stick together! Much to his sister's dismay, he still didn't recognize me. He knew all the fast girls though. I guess I was just too saved looking for him to even have noticed. Back-then he was not even saved. Eeelch.

Well he had been through his changes having left the church and becoming a *bad boy*, selling drugs and doing time. He was once named in Fort Greene as Archie-Outlaw. That is his story and I will let him tell it but by the time he called me he was back, saved, working in his father's church and studying to be an Emergency Medical Technician.

By the end of the phone call, we had arranged a meeting. He would come to New Life Tabernacle after his class and we would meet face-to-face. He came. We met. The choir never did sing at his anniversary and it was the beginning of our destiny together.

Being busy is not such a good thing sometimes. I almost lost my man running around the place. I had misplaced his number and I couldn't believe how crazy I was trying to find it. I could care less about others. He would call me and leave a message on my machine but never left his number. I was bugging out. I tried looking him up in the directory but was misspelling his last name as "McGuinness". Soon he had stopped calling and I was so upset. But God had another plan!

I really believed this was a God-thing because I had been in a place of spiritual renewal. I had gotten out of the will of God and everything in my life had been affected. I had begun to lose my favor, I had lost my job which would never have bothered me before because, like Samson, I'd shake myself and the Lord would bless me again with another great job; but not this time, I had been blacklisted from the computer departments at Wall Street and things were not looking good.

I knew what the problem was. I was out of the will of God and enjoying the pleasures of sin but I also knew how to get back! I had begun to pray and I promised God, "No more tricks". I had seen the hand-writing on the wall and knew I had to get back to the place in God that I belonged. I had never asked God for a husband until a day or two before I got that phone call. It had snowed and my car was covered in snow. I had to go to work so I grabbed a dust pan and planned to go out and knock the snow off of my car with it. It was at that moment when I looked around and noticed the women standing by while their husbands were removing snow from their cars and I muttered, "God, I need a husband!" I think he heard that.

I had a friend at New Life named Enid Dunlap who said that God told her to give me an appreciation service. I knew that was not a good idea because we didn't do that at New Life. Everyone had equal value and we were all so busy building that we didn't have time for that. Enid Dunlap was relentless and got Pastor Figueroa to agree to, *the friends and family of Evang. Cynthia Johnson invite you to a service of love and appreciation held at New Life Tabernacle.* That was on Saturday, January 27th 1991.

It was a spectacular night. That Enid Dunlap did her good work to get the place packed inside and out, upstairs and down; it was a fire hazard. They had to give the Fireman free fried chicken to leave us alone. Every choir in New York City was there. I had M.C.'d concerts for most if not all of them but still couldn't figure out how she got that place so packed.

This was one of the grandest days of my life and I wanted Pastor Batts to be there. Everyone at New Life knew of her. I spoke of her often. She consented to come and I sent her a round-trip ticket from Virginia. Although my First Lady was the scheduled speaker, by the time Pastor Batts got finished giving her remarks the place was going bananas! She had a way of knowing just what to say. Although she had grown significantly older, she was still anointed, still sharp and still a fire-starter. There was no need for preaching after that. We bucked a while.

It was offering time when I could finally see to the back of the church. (The church still thins out at offering time. The tight people go downstairs to eat chicken, hang out and fellowship until giving time is over.) In the corner, near the back of the church I saw him! Archie McInnis was in the building. Cheese grin! He was with a girl but I didn't care. I waited patiently until he gave his offering; all of those who gave had to pass by me to get back to their seats. I hugged all of my well wishers as they passed by. The line went on forever but here he was! He smiled and reached out for a hug. I held up the whole line. I hugged him a long time and whispered, "How come you don't leave your

106

number when you call?" He said, "Because I already gave you my number. I figured you didn't call because you weren't interested, so I moved on." I said, "Who's that girl you're with?" he said, "She's just a friend; a sister in the Lord". I said, "Well, find out how she's getting home because you're going out to eat with me O.K.?" Now, don't judge me. I had lost him once and wasn't planning on losing him again! Don't judge me.

We became friends, more than friends. I was in love with him and he was in love with me. We talked every day and all night long on the phone. We met after our services and went to church, to the movies and to restaurants together. What clinched it for me was the night our church had gone all the way to New Jersey for service and finished very late at night but I made my way to Fort Greene just to see him. When I was driving my car down Myrtle Avenue I had a moment, what in the world was I doing? I would never have done this before! I remembered my First Lady's words, "When he comes, you'll know him because you'll do for him what you won't do for any other." Like Neo from the Matrix, he was the one!

Archie was saved for real. He did not live a double life. He had a holiness conviction and he served God with every fiber of his being. There were no hidden secrets. No habits. No perversions. He was honest and trustworthy.

Let me digress here to share why those things were so very important to me. Since I got saved as a young girl, I cannot say that I was saved from a miserable life of sin. Most, if not all, of the sin I

107

learned how to commit, I learned from church people. I had regular involvement with ministers who drank alcohol regularly, I know people who leave church and go to clubs, I've met married people who cheat on their spouses regularly with ease and little obvious conviction, I know of people who go both ways, bisexuals and homosexuals, musicians who play better high than sober, pornography addicts and pedophiles and they all claimed to be saved. While I am not slam-dunking anyone in judgment and I have an appreciation for God's mercy and his grace, especially because I was all in it myself, and while I know there's blood for all of that, I surely didn't want to marry it. It was important for me to see examples of victorious, holy living and to know that the power of the Holy Ghost still worked. I needed assurance that there really was a balm in Gilead and that it really worked.

I'm not just talking about churches with no apparent, "standard"; I've met freaks of the week in Holiness churches! They preach holiness and sleep with little kids or buy prostitutes, lie and steal – so it's not the church that needs a standard, it's the individual believer who needs a personal relationship with Christ for real. If you are not careful and the majority of your relationships are not victorious you just might start to believe that holy living is impossible and everybody is into something. It was important for me to know that Archie didn't have any game about him.

From January to July, 1991 we were inseparable. He was always there and I was always glad. He loved me and he showed me. He passed my checklist; full of the Holy Ghost, good looking, no baby-mamas, good-looking, no bad-habits, good-looking great holy parents who had been married as long as I was alive, good looking and no bad credit. In fact, he had no credit and no job but a brother had potential. He was almost finished his E.M.T training and would be an Emergency Medical Technician and that was good enough for me.

Check it, on August 7, 1991 – six months later we went to the Justice of the Peace and got married. We just up and decided to do it when we realized we did not have any reason to wait. We only told his mother who happily came along, camera in hand and his friend, Dalvin who was our witness. We were cracking up laughing so hard we couldn't even kiss when the judge said, "You may kiss the bride." We both said at the same time, "We're crazy." I should have known then that our life would be filled with spontaneous excitement and never a dull moment. When Archie saw that the judge was a woman he immediately said, "We will have to do this again, I ain't getting married by no woman judge." Don't judge him; that was his truth.

We were not thinking about politics at the time. We were just happy and in love. We talked about whose church we would attend and decided to leave things as they were. What was simple for us, turned out to be a big deal for others. When the word finally got out, and we announced our engagement to be married on Saturday, December 7th (although we were already married) everybody started asking me if I was going to leave my church and go to his. It was such a big deal but not to us, at least for a while.

Even at our wedding, the talk of the town was about me staying at New Life or leaving. My pastor didn't even come down to the reception because they were having a round table discussion about a man leaving his mother and father and cleaving to his wife. I hadn't thought about all of that and could care less. It was my wedding day and I just wanted people to be happy for us.

After about 2 years or so, it started to kick in that we had divided loyalties and two-different churches may not have been such a good idea. The notion put a strain on our relationship and we were always arguing about it. After-church was difficult for us. It was difficult for me at my church because I was absent more often, trying to keep up with both church schedules. On New Year's Eve, I'd rush out early to be with my husband. I was reluctant but willing to leave New Life Tabernacle and join my father-in-law's church, New Life Pentecostal Holiness Church but after having a meeting with Bishop McInnis, I shared with my husband that I would be required to obey the rules of his father's church in order to stay. I would not be in rebellion but I would conform without complaint. I wanted peace in our home and I knew Jesus for myself. I could serve God in any church. I was past not wearing make-up and pants and me, nor my 1 year old daughter, would be allowed to wear them. We also could not go into movie theaters. These were simple things that didn't make or break me. I would conform.

My husband heard me out but refused to let me join. He was not comfortable with much of the legalism and did not want me to be subjected to it. He said we would pray about it. Surely if both of us pray to the same God, we should get the same answer.

Before you begin to judge my father-in-law, please know that this is his truth. I respect him greatly for standing by his principles and not compromising what he believes. To me those things were only cosmetic and I could definitely live without it in obedience and I was willing to do that. For the most part we were in agreement about the things that really mattered most. The principles of salvation bore no conflict.

Eventually, in October of 1996, during New Life Tabernacle's 10th Pastoral Anniversary, My husband told me that the Lord spoke to him and told him to leave his dad's church and join New Life Tabernacle. That was very difficult to grasp. It was a sad and painful time for him and his family. People were hurt and disappointed but I knew my husband, if he said it was God, it was God. He would not make an emotional move.

By then we had Chelsea who was 5 years old; born, December 25, 1992 and had just had Tre, Archie L. McInnis, III. We would have our last child, Aaron 1 year later on September 30, 1997. We were one family in one church; loyal to one God and one pastor but we continued to fellowship with NLPHC as often as we could. It was painful but necessary and the words of Pastor Batts came to mind again, "We will all know if it was a God-move in time." To this day I attest with absolute assurance that time is our ally! We should never let time become the enemy of our faith.

CHAPTER EIGHT
Full Effect Gospel Ministries

Archie and I served faithfully in New Life
Tabernacle. It was there that I saw my husband's
true calling and potential materialize. I saw in him a
deep-rooted devotion and loyalty as he served his
pastor closely. Often driving for him, carrying his
bags and serving in every area required. He was
faithful and dutiful, so much so, that his devotion to
Pastor Figueroa made me jealous. Very often,
although I understood it well, I would whine and
complain about him not helping me with the
children. What I really wanted to say but was too
proud and immature at the time to say was, "Babe, I
miss you and I want you to be here with me." If I
knew then what I know now what a mess of
arguments and fights could have been avoided!

Through it all I've seen my husband sow with tears
in his eyes. I've seen him give all that we had,
knowing that there was not much to eat at home but
he really believed God and had integrity. God
always made a way for us. He always provided
whatever we needed. He blessed my husband with a
great job that he didn't qualify for because he had a
B Felony. God provided all of our needs and my
husband provided all of my needs. He worked hard
and paid all the bills and kept our family well.

We worked together as a team to make sure we did
not go under. I worked and he worked and we were
stacking paper! We bought our first house in 1997
with faith and favor. He made certain that we never
missed an assessment or tithing during the time of

the purchase. Together we would declare that God is faithful.

Not long after joining New Life Tabernacle, my husband told me that the Lord had called him to Pastor and that the church would be called "Full Effect". He spoke to Pastor Figueroa who advised him to wait. He started Full Effect Crusade but it was short-lived. This would not be the traditional way for Archie- he would not start a crusade team that would evolve into a church. God would have Archie trust him from ground zero!

I began to see the divine providence of God. I started to look back over the years of my life and began to clearly see how God's hand was guiding my entire life. I would soon learn that it was all in his purpose, the verse "and we know that all things work together for good to them that love God, to them who are the called according to his purpose." Romans 8:28 – had come to life in my spirit. God knew I loved him and I knew he had called me according to his purpose. God was working his plan in our lives because both of us were *saved.*

Five years later, on July 27, 1998, after having spoken to our pastor, then, Bishop-designate, my husband was ordained an Elder and installed as Pastor of Full Effect Gospel Ministries.

Even though he waited five years as instructed, and even though the service was phenomenal and the power of God moved freely, and even though all things were done in order, I cannot tell you that the transition was easy.

It felt like we were abandoning our pastor. He felt as if he was losing us forever. Many things were said about Archie McInnis and even more about me but Pastor Batts' words rang true again, "time will tell if this is God". I've learned the importance of giving time a chance and not being quick to make final judgments.

I was married to a pastor after only seven years of marriage. I wasn't wise enough to see this *seven* as God's perfect number of completion and in hind-site the first of several sevens to come. (Married August, 1991 started church July, 1998; Seven years. 2005 we burned the mortgage on our 2nd church location; Seven years. 2013 purchased Allentown, PA Cathedral; another seven years.)

Although we faced our challenges, had our fights, suffered our seasons of craziness, we were both growing and learning and our marriage had purpose and the purpose had become much bigger than ourselves. It was bigger than our personal happiness. My husband had a plan for his family and I was on board with his plan. Together, we worked the plan.

He continued to work on his job at the NYC Department of Sanitation, while caring for his family and pastoring his church. My life was constantly changing. I had babies, a job and was trying to figure out how to be a wife and a First Lady. It really wasn't that difficult when we had no members, "First" lady meant, be the first to do whatever had to be done.

My husband said the Lord told him to start the
church in the basement of our home and we did.
That meant we had people in our house three times
a week. We also had a food pantry once a week and
all kinds of people were in and out of our house. As
the church grew, there were more and more people
all over the house, very often.

I cooked for the people, and we sold dinners to raise
money, we went to work, did laundry, burped the
babies and did ministry; It was our life. We fought
about everything but when it came to the business
of ministry, we worked together like a machine.

I can honestly tell you that we were so busy doing
ministry that we didn't have a lot of time for a lot of
things but Archie made sure we went on vacation,
enjoyed the children and he always bought me
beautiful gifts. He assured me of his love often and
promised me a good life if I'd stick with him.

It turned out that I had married a keen businessman!
Shoot! Who knew? He had learned much from
watching Bishop Figueroa, Bishop Billings and
others and managed the ministry finances well. The
Lord was blessing us and time would show that
surely this had been the Lord's doing.

Now, at fifty-two years old, with one church in two
states, members who love and respect us, several
properties, assets, three healthy children who work
closely in ministry and nearly 24 years of marriage,
I can quote the hymnist, "Great is thy faithfulness,
great is thy faithfulness, morning by morning, new
mercies I see, all I have needed, thy hand has
provided, great is thy faithfulness, Lord unto me.

CHAPTER NINE
What's the Point?

Some call it being born-again others prefer the term "saved" – it is the same action but a different term. My attempt in writing this book is to show the true super-natural nature of this action. My life has been a series of circumstances that appear to be coincidental and only time reveals the super-natural nature of them all.

I want you to know that even a dire child-hood existence does not terminate a super-natural plan of God for your life. To those who are experiencing what appears to be hell-on-earth, I say, get saved. It is not until you have given your life to Christ that his plan can unfold in your life.

To those whose life seems to be going just great, I say, get saved. It can only get better. It is not until you are saved that you come to understand your true, God-given purpose in this life. It is not until then that you have the power to overcome sin and Satan. Until then, every one of us is subject to the limitations of our flesh and at any time given over to the will of Satan. "Oooooh creepy!" you might say, but consider this; how does a good man, great father, keen businessman get strung out on Cocaine and lose it all? How does a perfect voice, delightful entertainer, million-dollar movie star end up dead in a bathtub from an overdose of drugs? How does the perfect mom, faithful wife charming friend get caught up in an extramarital love triangle and end up shot to death? How does the preacher who electrified audiences and, through his ministry, drew countless souls to Christ end up on his front porch murdered by his own hand? You would conclude that nobody planned these endings for their lives but you would be wrong. Satan has a plan for our lives just like Christ does!

The truth is, bad things happen to good people but I will not use that as an out for Satan. I will not denounce his cunning handiwork for the things I cannot explain. He is described in Scripture as a roaring lion, seeking whom he may devour. If you play with his stuff he takes ownership of your soul even if it means he puts you on top of the world. Superstars, who live extremely lavish lives with more money than they can spend in ten lifetimes, have often confessed to "selling their souls" to Satan. He became lord of their lives and when they tried to denounce him he destroyed them by their own lusts.

Whenever someone faces an untimely death of a loved one, a natural response is, "God's will was done" or "why did God take my loved one away from me", "how can a loving God allow such tragedies?" I've never heard anyone say – "this person lived for Satan and Satan destroyed them." We sing and funeralize everyone into the hands of a loving Savior while Satan laughs at our need to be comforted. If we denounce Satan and his deeds and declare that if you live by the sword you shall die by the sword and offer people an alternative life-style instead of making them believe that everybody will end up in heaven after the choir sings the last song at the funeral, it is possible that we will save others from damnation.

"Killer Joe", "Murderer" and "Cold Blood" are fictitious names for gang-bangers who went on heartless murdering sprees for respect; killing children, innocent by-standers and rival gang members; These cats are being used by Satan! The Nigerian rebels, who terrorize the nation with gruesome murdering campaigns are being used by Satan! The politicians who sanctioned the idea that poor people should be grouped together in public housing and forced into a life-style of, *survival of the fittest,* has been used by Satan! It is Satan that intercepts the subconscious minds of boys and girls and causes them to believe they are attracted to those of the same sex – so attracted that they change their appearances, risk their lives in sexual promiscuity and destroy family relationships. It is Satan who causes a woman to fall in love with her dog and have sex with him in private.

God did not release the diseases associated with these acts! Satan did! What does he do? He gets people to become actively involved in that which has been prohibited by God and then gets them to blame God for the destructive repercussions! He will get you to curse God and die destroying all hope for your eternal life.

Can you tell by now that I hate him? He is a deceiver; a snake by nature and he has been doing his dirty work since time began. He has even deceived the good Christians into believing that life is all about getting by. Just be happy! Find a spouse, raise a family and be a good moral saint then die and go to heaven, ignoring him while he wreaks havoc all around us.

He is a deceiver. He gets preachers and pastors to sell out to the lime-light only to increase the wattage on them when they fall! He gets people to denounce God because of the sins and indiscretions of one preacher who fell for his deceit. He wants the world to believe that there is no balm in Gilead and that true holiness is a figment of the imagination.

If I can help someone see Satan for who he is, I believe we can see God for who He is. We are all left to our own wills and make choices in life based on our belief systems and our desires but also based on supernatural suggestions. Those who give their lives to Christ get better suggestions, those who do not, get deception.

Mine is not, by far, the perfect life, neither do I claim to be faultless. I've shared, without too many details, the many challenges I've faced and continue to face on this journey, yet through it all, God's faithfulness and his hand of providence remains consistent. Everything I've ever needed, God has supplied.

I deliberately did not write this book from the perspective of a high-powered Evangelist, Debonair First Lady nor a distinguished Doctor of Divinity but I wrote it from the perspective of the young girl whose life was supernaturally changed by the power of a real God through real salvation.

Perhaps after having read this book, someone who has been sitting on a church pew or a park bench wondering what in the world was going wrong in his life, will get a revelation.

Perhaps a Christian who has found himself living
without power to change has made a determination
to find God for real and seek Christ for salvation or
maybe a choir member who sings the Gospel will
truly embrace this Christianity as a culture, as a
lifestyle.

I don't know but it is my desire that we all come to
know Christ for who he is; rebuking all carnality
and political agendas and that we are certain that
our lives are not lived according to the system of
this world but according to the will of God.

In conclusion I will offer several simple prayers
based on the many diverse circumstances we might
find ourselves in today. I believe that if you have
read this book, up to this point, something has been
in it for you. Choose the appropriate prayer and say
it out loud in your prayer time as often as you need
to say it.

****

Prayer for Salvation - New Convert

Dear Jesus, I come to you now to accept you as
Lord of my life. I don't know everything but I
know enough to know that I need you in my life. I
believe that you are the Savior of the world. I
believe that you died for the sins of the world and I
believe you came back from the dead to prove it.
Satan has deceived me. I have sinned against you
and I repent. I am Godly and intently sorry for all
of my sins and I ask you now to please forgive me.
Come now into my life and save me. Your word
says, *For if thou shalt confess with thy mouth the*

Lord Jesus, and shalt believe in thine heart that God hath raised him from the dead, thou shalt be saved. So today, right now, I confess that I am saved and I thank you for saving me. Amen

Prayer for Restoration – Backslider

Dear Jesus I come to you now to recommit my life to you. I have strayed away from you. I have denied your word and was drawn away by my own desires. I walked away from your presence and sought my own will. I'm sorry. I want to come back home to your will for my life. Take me back, dear Lord, to the place where I first received you. Your word says, "Turn, O backsliding children, saith the Lord; for I am married unto you:" So I thank you for restoration now. I thank you for restoring my soul In Jesus name, Amen.

Prayer for Deliverance

Dear Jesus I know you. I love you and I desire to please you. I ask you right now for deliverance from the stronghold that Satan has over my mind. I need to be free from the bondage of perpetual sin and I ask you for complete and total deliverance today. Lord I trust you to remove unsanctified desires from my heart and my mind in Jesus name. Lord, fill me with your Holy Spirit and let your power fall on me now. I release myself to your power because I cannot do this on my own. Help me now Jesus to understand your word because faith comes by hearing your word. Give me understanding and strengthen me now, In Jesus name, Amen.

Prayer for the Inner-filling of the Holy Spirit

Dear Jesus, I thank you for saving my soul. I thank you for sanctifying my spirit through your word. Now Lord, I pray that you would fill me with your Holy Spirit as you did on the Day of Pentecost. I realize that I cannot do your will without the help of your Holy Spirit. I release myself to your power now. Fall fresh upon me and fill me with your power. Baptize me now with the fire of your Holy Spirit and let it live in me today and always in Jesus name, Amen.

■■

There is no need to pray for health, wealth or material things now because you have done the hard part! The Bible says, "But see ye first the kingdom of God, and his righteousness; and all these things shall be added unto you." Matthew 6:33

If you have prayed any one of these prayers, your next step is to make sure you attend a Bible believing ministry for prayer and study.

Let me warn you; you have just frustrated the plan of Satan for your life. He is very angry but can only do to you what you allow. He will try but know this, "No weapon that is formed against thee shall prosper; and every tongue that shall rise against thee in judgment thou shalt condemn. This is the heritage of the servants of the Lord; and their righteousness is of me, saith the Lord." (Isaiah 54:17)

Let me share that good development comes from good nurturing. Your spiritual development relies on nurturing from the word of God that is rightly divided and full of supernatural power. If you are not in a ministry that is causing you to develop properly, please consider coming to where I am! Full Effect Gospel Ministries is one church in two states at the time of this writing. Feel free to visit our website at www.effect900.com for more information.

John 3

King James Version (KJV)

3 There was a man of the Pharisees, named Nicodemus, a ruler of the Jews:

[2] The same came to Jesus by night, and said unto him, Rabbi, we know that thou art a teacher come from God: for no man can do these miracles that thou doest, except God be with him.

[3] Jesus answered and said unto him, Verily, verily, I say unto thee, Except a man be born again, he cannot see the kingdom of God.

[4] Nicodemus saith unto him, How can a man be born when he is old? can he enter the second time into his mother's womb, and be born?

[5] Jesus answered, Verily, verily, I say unto thee, Except a man be born of water and of the Spirit, he cannot enter into the kingdom of God.

[6] That which is born of the flesh is flesh; and that which is born of the Spirit is spirit.

[7] Marvel not that I said unto thee, Ye must be born again.

[8] The wind bloweth where it listeth, and thou hearest the sound thereof, but canst not tell whence it cometh, and whither it goeth: so is every one that is born of the Spirit.

[9] Nicodemus answered and said unto him, How can these things be?

[10] Jesus answered and said unto him, Art thou a master of Israel, and knowest not these things?

[11] Verily, verily, I say unto thee, We speak that we do know, and testify that we have seen; and ye receive not our witness.

[12] If I have told you earthly things, and ye believe not, how shall ye believe, if I tell you of heavenly things?

[13] And no man hath ascended up to heaven, but he that came down from heaven, even the Son of man which is in heaven.

[14] And as Moses lifted up the serpent in the wilderness, even so must the Son of man be lifted up:

[15] That whosoever believeth in him should not perish, but have eternal life.

[16] For God so loved the world, that he gave his only begotten Son, that whosoever believeth in him should not perish, but have everlasting life.

¹⁷ For God sent not his Son into the world to condemn the world; but that the world through him might be saved.

¹⁸ He that believeth on him is not condemned: but he that believeth not is condemned already, because he hath not believed in the name of the only begotten Son of God.

¹⁹ And this is the condemnation, that light is come into the world, and men loved darkness rather than light, because their deeds were evil.

²⁰ For every one that doeth evil hateth the light, neither cometh to the light, lest his deeds should be reproved.

²¹ But he that doeth truth cometh to the light, that his deeds may be made manifest, that they are wrought in God.

²² After these things came Jesus and his disciples into the land of Judaea; and there he tarried with them, and baptized.

²³ And John also was baptizing in Aenon near to Salim, because there was much water there: and they came, and were baptized.

²⁴ For John was not yet cast into prison.

²⁵ Then there arose a question between some of John's disciples and the Jews about purifying.

²⁶ And they came unto John, and said unto him, Rabbi, he that was with thee beyond Jordan, to

whom thou barest witness, behold, the same baptizeth, and all men come to him.

27 John answered and said, A man can receive nothing, except it be given him from heaven.

28 Ye yourselves bear me witness, that I said, I am not the Christ, but that I am sent before him.

29 He that hath the bride is the bridegroom: but the friend of the bridegroom, which standeth and heareth him, rejoiceth greatly because of the bridegroom's voice: this my joy therefore is fulfilled.

30 He must increase, but I must decrease.

31 He that cometh from above is above all: he that is of the earth is earthly, and speaketh of the earth: he that cometh from heaven is above all.

32 And what he hath seen and heard, that he testifieth; and no man receiveth his testimony.

33 He that hath received his testimony hath set to his seal that God is true.

34 For he whom God hath sent speaketh the words of God: for God giveth not the Spirit by measure unto him.

35 The Father loveth the Son, and hath given all things into his hand.

[36] He that believeth on the Son hath everlasting life: and he that believeth not the Son shall not see life; but the wrath of God abideth on him.

Amen

Made in the USA
Middletown, DE
21 September 2023

38920507R00080